LEARN C THROUGH STORIES

C Programming Skills — From Basic to Master

Version 1.53

Muru Theivasegamani

Dedication

To my greatly respected teachers,

Thiru R. Chinnaswamy (RC), Thiru K. Sriramulu (KS) and Thiru C. Kandasamy (CK),

and to all my teachers whose guidance, knowledge and encouragement contributed to the person I became and to whatever success I have achieved.

With gratitude and respect.

Muru Theivasegamani

"Knowledge becomes powerful when it is understood, experienced, improved and shared for human learning and social progress."

Understood → Experienced → Improved → Shared → Human Learning → Social Progress

An INDHEA Learning Series

Learn • Build • Share

Why Learn C in the Age of Artificial Intelligence?

Artificial Intelligence is changing the way we use computers and develop software. This naturally raises a question: Why should a learner study programming when AI can already generate programs?

My answer is simple, learning programming is not only about learning how to write code. It develops logical thinking, problem-solving skills, and an understanding of how instructions, data and computers work together.

AI can help us create a program, but the ability to understand the problem, evaluate the solution, identify mistakes and improve the result still requires human understanding. A learner with a strong foundation in programming can therefore use AI more effectively than someone who treats it merely as a tool that produces answers.

This book begins with C because the objective is not simply to teach a programming language. It is to help the learner think like a programmer.

Why Another Book on C?

Thousands of books already teach C programming. So, why write another one? Because this book attempts to teach it differently.

Human learning becomes more meaningful when new information can be connected with something we already understand. An isolated fact may be difficult to remember, but ideas connected through context, experience and association can become easier to understand and recall.

Instead of presenting C as a sequence of commands, definitions and programs**, Learn C Through Stories** connects programming concepts through a continuing story Character encounter problem, discuss them, attempt solutions, make mistakes, test their programs, debug them and improve what they have built.

The story therefore is not merely decoration around the programming lessons. It is part of the learning method.

This approach was influenced in part by what I learned while studying Applied Psychology and by my interest in how association, experience and context contribute to human learning.

My hope is that learners will not merely remember C syntax. They will remember why a concept became necessary, where they used it, what went wrong, how they corrected it, and what they learned from the experience.

How to Use This Book?

This is not a book where you simply memorize programming commands. You will learn C through a continuing story in which learners observe real problems, think about solutions, write programs, test them, discover mistakes, debug them and improve the result.

- Observe the problem before writing code
- Think about what the program must do
- Build the solution step by step
- Treat mistakes as opportunities to learn
- Use positive and negative test cases
- Understand why a correction works
- Improve a working solution when new requirements appear

The examples begin with deliberately limited assumptions so that each new programming concept can be learned clearly. As the story progresses, those assumptions are questioned and the program becomes more useful and more general.

The Learning Journey

PROBLEM → THINK → CODE → TEST → FIND → FIX → LEARN → IMPROVE

PROBLEM — Understand what needs to be solved.

THINK — Plan the logic before typing code.

CODE — Build the solution in small, understandable steps.

TEST — Try both expected and unexpected inputs.

FIND — Identify defects, limitations and unclear assumptions.

FIX — Correct the program and test it again.

LEARN — Understand why the problem occurred and why the correction works.

IMPROVE — Extend the solution when new needs or better ideas appear.

Acknowledgements

This book grew from a simple idea: programming becomes easier to understand when learners can connect each concept to a problem, experience the result, make mistakes, test their thinking and improve the solution.

During the review, editorial development and publishing preparation of Version 1.53, I used **ChatGPT by OpenAI** as an AI-assisted review, learning and publishing partner. It assisted me in refining the language, reviewing the structure and technical explanations, improving the learning flow from a reader's perspective, and understanding and preparing for the self-publishing process, including book formatting, ISBN application and publication planning.

The original concept, story, characters, teaching methodology and programming approach were developed by the author. All suggestions and revisions were reviewed and accepted by the author, who retains full responsibility for the final content and publication.

Publication Information

Title: *Learn C Through Stories*

Subtitle: *C Programming Skills — From Basic to Master*

Version: 1.53

Author: Murugesan Theivasegamani

Author Credentials: B.Sc. (Computer Science), M.Sc. (Computer Science), MBA, M.E. (Computer Science and Engineering), M.Sc. (Applied Psychology)

Publisher: Self-Published

ISBN: 978-93-344-7219-6

Edition: First Self-Published Publication Edition

Contents

PART I — A PROBLEM WORTH SOLVING

A Project with a Purpose

It was a long weekend, with Friday being a holiday for Vinayakar Chathurthi. Indu, Bubesh and Harsha were discussing their project during a conference call. The conversation went on for quite some time.

Many subjects and topics came up one after another, but they still could not settle on a convincing project idea. They also had an additional goal: their project needed to be unique and capable of earning them good marks. However, the discussion diverted toward upcoming movies and Pooja, and the day finally ended without them achieving their goal.

Saturday morning was pleasant at Marina Beach after about 3 cm of rain late on Friday night. The sky was clear, and the reddish sun slowly changed its appearance as it rose. A cool breeze from the Bay of Bengal made the morning even more refreshing.

Near the Lighthouse, Indu, Bubesh and Harsha met Thea, Indu's elder sister and their senior, after their morning cycling. About a hundred metres away, a small crowd had gathered. People were laughing and making fun of someone.

"What is going on there?" asked Bubesh.

"No idea. Let us go and see," Thea replied.

All four approached the crowd and noticed that two of their school seniors, who were also Thea's classmates, were trying to fly a small model helicopter. It failed again and again. Each time it fell, the surrounding crowd laughed, making the two students more frustrated.

Thea observed the helicopter carefully. This attempt was better than the previous one: it climbed a little higher, but again fell towards the left. She replaced a light pin on the right side with a one-rupee coin, adding a little more weight. The helicopter flew successfully.

The seniors were delighted and thanked her.

One of them asked, "Hey, how did you find the solution?"

"The helicopter kept falling towards the left. That suggested that its weight was not balanced. I added a little weight on the other side to balance it. It was a small change," Thea replied.

"How did we miss it? Are we dumb?" another student asked emotionally.

Thea replied, "No, not at all. If you were dumb, you could not have assembled this helicopter. The problem was that the people around you were laughing, and that distracted you. Each failure increased the pressure, so you became more focused on making it fly than on understanding why it was falling".

"Then what did you do differently from us?" he asked.

“I was neither influenced by the crowd nor trying to prove anything. I simply observed what the helicopter was doing. That helped me identify the possible cause. In life, our attempts to learn are often affected when we become too concerned about what other people think.”

She continued, “Losing focus while learning or listening can happen to anyone. It is part of human behaviour, and it can happen to me too. When we notice it, we should try to bring our attention back to the problem”.

“Every laugh pulled both of you deeper into the pressure. I was outside that pressure, so I could observe the helicopter more calmly. Sometimes, stepping away from the urge to succeed immediately helps us see the problem more clearly.”

The students thanked her and began packing their helicopter equipments.

Harsha whispered to Indu and Bubesh, “I think Thea may be able to give us a clue for our project. Shall we ask her?”

They all agreed. Bubesh began, “Thea, we are also doing a group project. We have discussed many ideas, but we still have not finalized a topic. We have to submit the project title by Monday, and we have only two days left. Can you help us?”

Thea asked, “What is your focus area?”

“We discussed many ideas. One shortlisted idea is to assemble a windmill that generates power through a dynamo and lights a set of LEDs. But getting the components is a little difficult,” they explained.

“What will your role be in this project?” Thea asked.

Indu explained their simple objective: “We will buy the components, assemble them and submit the project. It will be different from what the other students do, and we may get good marks.”

Thea replied, “Marks should not be the real objective of a project, especially a group project. In the future, all of you will work as members of teams. A project should help you learn how to contribute, solve problems and work together. Marks can follow the learning.”

Bubesh said, “Yes, you are right. Shall we make the same helicopter?”

Thea replied, “It is not as easy as it looks. They have been working on it for months because they want to become aeronautical engineers. They are learning through something connected with their own interest. What do you want to become?”

“Computer Engineers,” all three replied immediately.

“Good. Then try to write a useful computer program,” said Thea.

“What sort of program?” Harsha asked.

"If I tell you everything, what will be left for you to discover? But make sure that the program is useful enough to justify the effort you put into it. A program is not valuable merely because it runs; it should solve a real problem."

They understood the value of her guidance. After discussing it as a team, they decided to meet their class teacher after breakfast.

They also noticed something interesting. The same crowd that had been laughing half an hour earlier was now appreciating the seniors and asking questions about the helicopter. The three friends wondered how quickly people's reactions could change after success.

All three decided to meet CK Sir, their class teacher, who lived near the Government Library. Since it was a school holiday, they hoped he would be at home and free to guide them.

After breakfast, they went to their class teacher's house. As they parked their bicycles, a Rajapalayam dog named Gooch frightened them with a loud bark. CK Sir came out and welcomed them inside.

Observe Before You Program

They entered his office room and found him busy with work. His table was covered with answer sheets, a calculator, pens, pencils, an eraser and other materials.

Indu asked, "Sir, we need your help to finalize our team project title. You look very busy. Shall we come back this afternoon?"

He replied, "I am preparing your class report cards for the quarterly examination. It is almost complete and should take only about thirty more minutes. Let me finish it quickly; then I can help you."

Soon, the pleasant aroma of coffee beans filled the room. Mrs. CK served them Kumbakonam filter coffee. They thanked her and enjoyed it. Refreshed, they began observing CK Sir's work carefully.

He took one student's report card and the answer sheets for all subjects. He entered the marks in the report card, calculated the total using a calculator, found the average, and entered the result and grade. He left the rank column blank and moved to the next student.

Harsha asked, "Sir, can we help you calculate the marks?"

CK Sir smiled and thanked him. "Even if you do some of the calculations, I will have to verify them again. That would still take nearly half the time, so your help may not reduce the work very much. But thank you for offering."

Indu asked, "Sir, how much time does this work usually take?"

He replied, “One student takes about three to four minutes, and there are fifty students. So the whole class takes around three hours. Only five students are left now, so I should finish in about fifteen minutes.”

Bubesh asked, “Why don’t we make this our project and try to help our class teacher?” The three discussed the idea and agreed.

CK Sir finished his work, arranged the papers neatly on the shelves and turned to them.

Harsha said, “Sir, you spend several hours on this work every time. Can we replace some of this manual work with a computer program and improve the accuracy as well?”

CK Sir was very happy to hear the idea. “That would be useful. If you can computerize these repeated calculations and report preparation steps, it could save a significant amount of time”.

Indu asked, “What difficulties do you face while doing this work?”

“The main concern is accuracy. I have to avoid mistakes while doing the same calculations repeatedly. Otherwise, it is regular and routine work,” replied CK Sir.

CK Sir then asked, “How can I help you today?”

They explained why they had come: they wanted an idea for a useful computer project. After observing his work, they had decided to write a program that could reduce the repetitive manual effort involved in preparing student results.

CK Sir was impressed and appreciated their intention. He wished them success.

Turning Manual Work into Requirements

They went to the library, parked their bicycles and began discussing the next steps. First, they wrote down the teacher’s work in sequence.

Their computer teacher, RC Sir, came by and stopped when he saw his students.

“Good morning, sir,” all three said as they stood up.

“Good morning. What are you doing here?” he asked. Bubesh explained the story.

“Wow! It is great to hear that,” RC Sir said.

Indu said, “Sir, you taught us that before writing a program, we must first understand the problem. We have understood the basic need. Can you help us review the steps for our program?”

Harsha restated the work they had observed and recorded on paper.

1. CK Sir takes each student’s marks from the answer sheets for every subject and writes them in the report card against the corresponding subject.
2. He uses a calculator to add all the subject marks and writes the total in the Total column.

3. He calculates the total again to verify it. Then he finds the average by dividing the total by 5, because there are five subjects, and writes the average in the report.
4. Based on the student's marks, average and minimum pass criteria, he fills the Result column as PASS or FAIL.
5. The grade is awarded based on the defined grading criteria.
6. He leaves the Rank column blank initially and moves to the next student to repeat the same work.

"Wow! Nicely captured. This is important in programming, and the sequence is also important. Well done," RC Sir appreciated.

Indu added, "We missed one point. After completing the report cards, he arranges them based on total marks, keeping the highest score first in descending order. That is how the ranking can be prepared."

By observing these steps, they began to recognize a pattern in the work. A pattern here means that the same procedure is repeated for every student.

Total = Tamil + English + Maths + Science + Social
= 80 + 75 + 96 + 90 + 89
= 430
Average = Total / Number of Subjects
= 430 / 5
= 86 %
Referred to the Grade Sheet and found grade as A

They planned to develop the program gradually: first build the core solution, then add features around it as new requirements became clear. This incremental approach would help them learn from each working stage instead of trying to build everything at once.

Harsha asked, "Can we avoid entering all these details manually? That is also manual work, isn't it?"

RC Sir replied, "Yes, some manual entry can be reduced. Student details are usually entered only once. Marks could also be captured using other technologies, but that would require additional hardware, software and complexity. For this project, first focus on solving the main problem with the resources you already have."

Indu said, "This is becoming interesting, sir. We have learned C programming, but we may need your help during the project. We are going to start today."

RC Sir said, "Once you write this program, the idea could potentially be adapted for other classes too. That means the benefit is not limited to one teacher or one class, and it may save one man-month of effort for our school".

Cost, Benefit, Roles and Test Cases

Harsha asked, "Sir, what does 'man-month' means?"

RC Sir explained, "A man-month is a traditional project-estimation term for the amount of work one person might perform in about one working month. For a simple illustration, if we assume 8 working hours a day and about 21 working days in a month, that is roughly 168 working hours. But remember: saving 168 hours of repeated work does not automatically mean that one employee or one salary is removed. The real benefit may be that those hours can be used for more valuable work."

"So our program could save a large amount of teachers' time," Harsha said happily.

Harsha continued, "Thea called this the cost benefit of our work. So the time saved for the school is one of the benefits. Is that correct, sir?"

RC Sir replied, "Yes, time saved can be one benefit. But cost-benefit analysis compares the resources and effort required for a project with the benefits expected from it."

Bubesh asked, "When do we do this cost-benefit analysis?"

RC Sir replied, "Usually, we estimate the likely costs and benefits before starting a project, and we can review them again later using actual results. For example, if a software company charged □1,00,000 to develop a solution, the school would compare that cost with the time saved, improved accuracy, reuse across classes, and other benefits before deciding whether the investment was worthwhile. Based on our understanding, it will save one man-month of effort every two months. If so, an investment equivalent to a salary cost of □20,000 will be recovered by the fifth time. This means 5 × □20,000 = □1,00,000, which implies that the invested cost will be earned back after 10 months".

Indu said, "In our case, we are doing the project as part of our learning, and the teachers already have laptops. So, our direct project cost is very low".

RC Sir replied, "Correct, educational projects can often explore ideas at a lower direct cost because learning itself is one of the benefits. Commercial organizations, however, must also consider salaries, infrastructure, maintenance, support and many other costs."

He continued, "More importantly, if routine work is reduced, teachers can spend that time on student development. I will speak to Headmaster Sriramulu Sir and get the necessary guidance if your project reaches that stage."

"Thank you so much, sir," all three said warmly.

RC Sir said, "You are most welcome. Since you are working as a team, each of you should take a primary role. One can lead programming, another can represent the class teacher or user, and another can focus on testing. All of you can still contribute to every area."

Indu asked, "What are test cases, sir?"

RC Sir explained, "Suppose you enter one student's marks for five subjects. Before running the program, manually calculate the expected total, average, result and grade. Then run the program with the same marks and compare the output. That set of inputs and expected results becomes a test case."

"Other possible scenario may be students with

1. Mark with above 90% average
2. Mark with above 80% average
3. Like all other grades
4. Failed in one subject but rest or all high marks
5. Failed in all subjects
6. Student absent in one or more subjects

“Continue like this. These are examples of valid or positive test cases. You should also prepare negative test cases.”

Harsha asked, “What are negative test cases, sir?”

RC Sir replied, “Suppose you accidentally enter 150 instead of 50 for one subject, or enter a negative mark such as -33. Your program should recognize that the input is invalid and should not process it as a normal mark. Tests like these help you check how the program behaves with invalid input.”

RC Sir received a phone call from his son, who had finished his swimming class and was waiting to be picked up. RC Sir had to leave. The three students were very happy with what they had learned and thanked him warmly.

“As sir said, we need to choose our primary roles. Who is going to represent the class teacher?”

“I will,” Bubesh said happily.

Harsha added, “I am good at finding faults and testing. I will take the tester role.”

Indu said, “Then I will take the programmer role. Still, all three of us will work together and step into one another’s roles whenever needed. My laptop already has Visual Studio, so we can use it to start the program.”

They decided to meet at Indu’s house that evening and then returned home.

Indu went home and told her sister Thea about their new project. Thea said, “Very good. I appreciate the effort. It is useful, and it gives you many opportunities to develop the program gradually as you learn.”

Indu asked, “What is a software package?”

Thea explained, “A software package is more than a single piece of source code. A useful solution may contain the program itself along with supporting files, configuration, documentation and a way to install or deploy it. You do not need all of that now, but it is useful to understand that real software grows beyond one program file.”

She continued, “You have already learned many of the C concepts needed to begin this program. Ranking may require sorting logic, which can be a little more difficult, so leave that until the basic result processing works correctly.”

Indu shared the details with her project teammates through WhatsApp by creating a new group called "AimUP". They were excited and decided to revise what they had learned in their C programming classes.

The Structure of a Program

They placed their C programming book, computer classwork notebook, a new notebook for the project, a pen, pencil and eraser in front of God and offered a short prayer before beginning their work.

They recalled the basic structure of a C program from what they had learned in class and wrote a simple skeleton in their notebook.

Basic Structure of a C Program

```
#Libraries
..
int main(void)
{
        // variable declarations and initiation
        ......
        // body of program
        ......
        return 0;
}
```

"What does 'structure' mean? I have forgotten the definition," Indu asked.

They were not completely sure, so they asked Thea.

Thea replied, "Let us take the example of writing a formal letter to your class teacher. It normally follows an expected structure: DATE and PLACE, FROM, TO, SUBJECT, the message, and your signature."

"But why do we need such a structure when we are writing to our own class teacher? The teacher already knows who we are, and the content itself tells her what we need," one of them asked.

They could not think beyond that point and asked Thea to explain.

Thea said, "That may seem sufficient when you think only about yourself and your class teacher. But if the same letter goes through the school office, other people may need to understand who wrote it, whom it is for and what it is about. A standard structure makes the information easier to interpret."

She continued, "Programming is similar. A C program also follows rules and conventions so that the compiler can understand how the program is organized. Different development environments may create slightly different starting templates, but the underlying programming concepts remain the same."

IDE NOTE — The screenshots and some generated project code in this story come from a Visual Studio C++ console environment. The learners are using that environment as a convenient tool while focusing on C programming concepts. Where the IDE generates Microsoft-specific or C++-specific template code, the book will identify it clearly so that learners can distinguish the core C concepts from the development environment.

Indu created a console project in Visual Studio and showed the structure generated by that version of the IDE.

```
// CProg01.cpp : Defines the entry point for the console application.
//

#include "stdafx.h"
int _tmain(int argc, _TCHAR* argv[])
{
        return 0;
}
```

Thea explained, “This is the starting structure generated by this Visual Studio project template. Other IDEs and newer versions may show a simpler or different starting program. Do not worry about those differences now. We will focus on the C programming concepts and understand each part as it becomes necessary.”

CONCEPT — A compiler checks source code and translates it into lower-level code as part of building an executable program. The translation analogy below is only a learning aid; a compiler does more than translate words from one language to another.

Bubesh asked, “What is a compiler?”

Thea replied, “Imagine that I know only Tamil and travel to Delhi, where I lose my luggage. I need to give a complaint to a railway police officer who understands only Hindi. What should I do?”

Harsha replied, “You would need help from someone who knows both Tamil and Hindi. You could explain the problem in Tamil, and that person could translate it into Hindi for the officer.”

Thea said, “Good. A compiler is not exactly a human translator, but that analogy helps us begin. We write a program in a language such as C because it is easier for us to express instructions that way. The compiler checks and translates the source code into a form that can ultimately be executed by the computer.”

She continued, “The exact executable produced depends on the compiler, operating system, processor and other details. So a program compiled for one environment may need to be rebuilt for another. For now, it is enough to remember this: we write source code, the compiler processes it, and the computer runs the resulting program.”

Thea added, “You do not need to go deeper into compiler design now. Continue with your program.”

Compiler, Library and First Output

Indu compiled the program successfully. When she ran it, a console window appeared, but nothing meaningful was displayed because the program had not yet been told to print anything.

“Then let us add a message to display,” she said.

Indu added an output statement to display a welcome message.

```
// CProg01.cpp : Defines the entry point for the console application.
//

#include "stdafx.h"

int _tmain(int argc, _TCHAR* argv[])
{
        cout<<"W E L C O M E, ALL THE BEST for your Learning of C";

        return 0;
}
```

Indu compiled the program again, but this time the compiler reported an error:

```
error C2065: 'cout' : undeclared identifier
```

“What does this mean?” Harsha asked.

Bubesh said, “We added `cout`, but the compiler does not recognize it in the program as it stands. We may be missing the required library or declaration.”

“What is a library?” Harsha asked.

Thea replied, “Let us assume that you need to create a school map for providing induction program for newly joined students in the school. This induction program includes the school map to find out what facilities are available and where it is located, how do you access it? This is not only for accessing, in any emergency what will be exited to escape from any accident like fire accident or during earthquake. So, you need to study the school building, get help from teachers and students to create the school map. Next year it is going to be same process to repeat. If so, this year plan will be kept in the school library or office, so every year this document will be re-used.”.

Thea continued, “Like that repeated functions like **cout**, are already written by someone and kept in the standard library. Only you need to add the library and use it. Also, we initially wrote our program for pure C, but we are using C++ environment, so we replace **print** command with **cout**”.

Harsha added, “Yes, I remember this from my first program. We need to include the appropriate header and make the standard-library name available, as shown below.”

```
#include <iostream>
using namespace std;
```

They added the required header and namespace statement to the Visual Studio program.

```
// CProg01.cpp : Defines the entry point for the console application.
//

#include "stdafx.h"
#include <iostream>

using namespace std;

int _tmain(int argc, _TCHAR* argv[])
{
            cout<<"W E L C O M E, ALL THE BEST for your Learning of C";

            return 0;
}
```

The program now compiled successfully. They ran the executable and saw the following output:

```
W E L C O M E, ALL THE BEST for your Learning of C
```

Bubesh said, "Wow, it works! Let us develop the program further."

Variables, Data Types and Arithmetic

Harsha agreed. "Now we need to add marks for five subjects and calculate the total and average."

Harsha continued, "According to my test case: Tamil = 89, English = 76, Maths = 100, Science = 95, Social = 96. The expected total is 456 and the expected average is 91.2."

Indu updated the program. She introduced variables to store the five subject marks, the total and the calculated average.

She added, "In the book, we will highlight the lines that change whenever practical. That will help us focus on the new concept instead of repeatedly reading unchanged code."

```
#include "stdafx.h"
#include <iostream>

using namespace std;

int _tmain(int argc, _TCHAR* argv[])
{
            int Tam, Eng, Mat, Sci, Soc, Tot, Avg;

            cout<<"W E L C O M E, ALL THE BEST for your Learning of C";

            Tam = 89;
            Eng = 76;
            Mat = 100;
            Sci = 95;
            Soc = 99;

            Tot = Tam + Eng + Mat + Sci + Soc;
```

```
        Avg = Tot / 5;

        cout << "Total :" << Tot;
        cout << "Average : " << Avg;

        return 0;
    }
```

Bubesh asked, “I understand that a variable stores a value that may change while the program runs. But why are we using `int` for some values and `float` for another?”

Thea replied, “Think of a variable as a named container for a value. Indu, can you bring me some water to take my morning tablet?”

Indu brought her a glass of water.

Thea asked, “When I asked for water, Indu brought it in a glass. Why didn’t she bring it in a towel or a large jug?”

Bubesh replied, “A towel cannot hold water like a container, and you need only enough water to take the tablet. A glass is suitable; a large jug would be unnecessary.”

Thea smiled and replied, “Excellent answer. As Bubesh pointed out, I need only a little water to swallow the tablet, so there is no need for a large container such as a jug. In the same way, choosing a suitable data type means selecting the right kind of container for a value. In our program, `int` can hold whole numbers, `float` can hold numbers with fractional parts, and `char` can hold a character. Later, when we need to store several characters together, we will learn how arrays can help.”

Indu added, “Here we have variables for the five subject marks, the total and the average. Their values can change when different marks are processed.”

Thea commented, “There is something important to notice about the data types. Let us see whether Harsha’s test case reveals it.”

Indu compiled and ran the program.

```
W E L C O M E, ALL THE BEST for your Learning of CTotal :456Average : 91
```

Harsha said, “The total matches my test case, but the average should be 91.2 and the program shows only 91. Also, everything appears on one line, so the output is difficult to read.”

Thea replied, “Good observation. `Avg` was declared as an `int`, so it stores a whole-number result and truncate fraction number. There is another issue too: if both operands of a division are integers, integer division is performed before the result is assigned. We need a floating-point calculation if we want a fractional average.”

Indu replied, “Yes, I see the problem. I will change the average to a floating-point type and make the division floating-point as well. I will also format the output with line breaks so that it is easier to read.”

She changed the program as shown below:

```
#include "stdafx.h"
#include <iostream>

using namespace std;

int _tmain(int argc, _TCHAR* argv[])
{
        int Tam, Eng, Mat, Sci, Soc, Tot;
        float Avg;

        cout<<"W E L C O M E, ALL THE BEST for your Learning of C";

        Tam = 89;
        Eng = 76;
        Mat = 100;
        Sci = 95;
        Soc = 96;

        Tot = Tam + Eng + Mat + Sci + Soc;

        Avg = Tot / 5.0;

        cout << "\nTotal :" << Tot;
        cout << "\nAverage : " << Avg;

        return 0;
}
```

She compiled and ran the program. The result was:

```
W E L C O M E, ALL THE BEST for your Learning of C
Total :456
Average : 91.2
```

Harsha approved it. "Yes, the result now matches my test case."

Bubesh added, "At the moment, we have to change the numbers in the source code and compile the program every time we want a new result. That is more work than using a calculator. According to our requirement, the program should accept the marks from the user, calculate the total and average, and display the individual subject marks as well."

Indu said, "That will be our next step."

She changed the program as shown below.

```
#include "stdafx.h"
#include <iostream>

using namespace std;

int _tmain(int argc, _TCHAR* argv[])
{
        int Tam, Eng, Mat, Sci, Soc, Tot;
        float Avg;
        cout<<"W E L C O M E, ALL THE BEST for your Learning of C";

        cin >> Tam;
```

```
        cin >> Eng;
        cin >> Mat;
        cin >> Sci;
        cin >> Soc;

        Tot = Tam + Eng + Mat + Sci + Soc;

        Avg = Tot / 5.0;

        cout << "\nTamil :" << Tot;
        cout << "\nEnglish :" << Tot;
        cout << "\nMaths :" << Tot;
        cout << "\nScience :" << Tot;
        cout << "\nSocial :" << Tot;

        cout << "\nTotal :" << Tot;
        cout << "\nAverage : " << Avg;

        return 0;
}
```

Harsha ran the program and entered the values from his test case. The program produced the following results:

```
W E L C O M E, ALL THE BEST for your Learning of C
89
76
100
95
96
Tamil :456
English :456
Maths :456
Science :456
Social :456
Total :456
Average : 91.2
```

Bubesh added, “This is better, Indu, but a new user will not know which subject mark to enter first or what comes next. We know the order because we wrote the program, but someone else should not have to discover it by making mistakes. The program should prompt the user with the subject name before each mark is entered.”

Indu noted the point, added prompts before each input, and compiled the program successfully.

```
#include "stdafx.h"
#include <iostream>

using namespace std;

int _tmain(int argc, _TCHAR* argv[])
{
        int Tam, Eng, Mat, Sci, Soc, Tot;
        float Avg;

        cout<<"W E L C O M E, ALL THE BEST for your Learning of C";

        cout << "\nEnter Tamil mark :";
        cin >> Tam;
        cout << "\nEnter English mark :";
        cin >> Eng;
        cout << "\nEnter Maths mark :";
```

```
            cin >> Mat;
            cout << "\nEnter Science mark :";
            cin >> Sci;
            cout << "\nEnter Social mark :";
            cin >> Soc;

            Tot = Tam + Eng + Mat + Sci + Soc;

            Avg = Tot / 5.0;

            cout << "\nTamil :" << Tot;
            cout << "\nEnglish :" << Tot;
            cout << "\nMaths :" << Tot;
            cout << "\nScience :" << Tot;
            cout << "\nSocial :" << Tot;

            cout << "\nTotal :" << Tot;
            cout << "\nAverage : " << Avg;

            return 0;
    }
```

Harsha ran the program and obtained the following output:

```
W E L C O M E, ALL THE BEST for your Learning of C
Enter Tamil mark :89
Enter English mark :76
Enter Maths mark :100
Enter Science mark :95
Enter Social mark :96
Tamil :456
English :456
Maths :456
Science :456
Social :456
Total :456
Average : 91.2
```

"It looks fine," Harsha said, and continued testing.

Thea stopped them. "Harsha, did you notice the subject marks in the output? Look carefully. Each subject is displaying the total instead of its own mark."

Harsha exclaimed, "Oh! I missed that."

Indu said, "Yes. I copied the output lines and forgot to replace `Tot` with the correct subject variable in each line."

Thea added, "This kind of mistake is common in software development. We may focus on one expected result—in this case, the total—and overlook other outputs such as the individual subject marks. Whenever you make a change, test the complete result, not just the part you changed. That is one reason careful testing is so important."

Indu corrected the output variables and compiled the program successfully.

```
#include "stdafx.h"
#include <iostream>

using namespace std;

int _tmain(int argc, _TCHAR* argv[])
```

```
{
        int Tam, Eng, Mat, Sci, Soc, Tot;
        float Avg;

        cout<<"W E L C O M E, ALL THE BEST for your Learning of C";

        cout << "\nEnter Tamil mark :";
        Tot = Tam + Eng + Mat + Sci + Soc;

        Avg = Tot / 5.0;

        cout << "\nTamil :" << Tam;
        cout << "\nEnglish :" << Eng;
        cout << "\nMaths :" << Mat;
        cout << "\nScience :" << Sci;
        cout << "\nSocial :" << Soc;

        cout << "\nTotal :" << Tot;
        cout << "\nAverage : " << Avg;

        return 0;
}
```

Harsha tested the corrected program. The output now matched the expectations.

```
W E L C O M E, ALL THE BEST for your Learning of C
Enter Tamil mark :89
Enter English mark :76
Enter Maths mark :100
Enter Science mark :95
Enter Social mark :96
Tamil :89
English :76
Maths :100
Science :95
Social :96
Total :456
Average : 91.2
```

Testing the First Result

This time Harsha was more careful. "I remember RC Sir telling us to test invalid inputs too. Let me try marks below 0 and above 100."

He deliberately entered invalid marks, including values below 0 and above 100.

```
W E L C O M E, ALL THE BEST for your Learning of C
Enter Tamil mark :189
Enter English mark :-1
Enter Maths mark :100
Enter Science mark :454
Enter Social mark :882
Tamil :189
English :-1
Maths :100
Science :454
Social :882
Total :1624
Average : 324.8
```

Validating Marks with Conditions

Harsha said, “The invalid-input tests failed. A subject mark should not be accepted if it is below 0 or above 100.”

Indu replied, “Yes. The program does not validate the input yet. We need a condition to detect an invalid mark.”

Harsha said, “I remember the idea of an `if` condition. It controls whether a statement is executed depending on whether a condition is true. For example, if my mother asks me to buy vegetables, she might say, ‘Buy tomatoes if the price is below a certain amount; otherwise, buy another vegetable.’”

Bubesh replied, “Exactly. A simple `if` statement looks like this:”

```
If( condition)
{
        // command 1
                ....
        // command n
}
```

Bubesh continued, “If the condition is true, the statement or block controlled by the `if` is executed. Braces are useful when we want the condition to control several statements.”

MISTAKE → TEST → DEBUG → LEARN

Indu added a first attempt at validating the Tamil mark:

```
cout << "\nEnter Tamil mark :";
cin >> Tam;
if(Tam <0 && Tam > 100)
        cout <<"\nEntered Tamil mark is incorrect";
```

Repeating Input with Loops

Bubesh stopped her. “Even if the condition detects an invalid mark, the program should ask again until the user enters a valid one. We need a loop.”

Thea added, “Good catch. A programmer should keep comparing the code with the expected behaviour. If a test fails, we return to the logic, understand the reason and correct it. Reviewing our own code is useful, but we can sometimes overlook mistakes because we already know what we intended to write. Another programmer may notice a logical error that we missed. Bubesh’s observation is a review comment, and it has helped Indu think about the requirement more carefully. That is the value of teamwork. Keep it up.”

Bubesh wrote the basic structure of a `while` loop.

```
while (condition) {
        // command 1
                ....
        // command n
}
```

Indu asked, “A **while** loop checks its condition before entering the loop. But here, we need to ask for a mark at least once and then decide whether to repeat. Would a **do...while** loop fit better?”

"Yes, the **do...while** loop operates a little differently from a **while** loop. A **while** loop checks the condition first and then executes the commands, whereas a **do...while** loop executes the commands first and checks the condition later. In this case, we get the first mark from the user and then check whether it is valid or not. Additionally, a loop continues until the condition fails. Therefore, we should use a **do...while** loop instead of a while loop."

Bubesh agreed and explained the functional structure of the **do...while** loop as shown below:

```
do {
        // command 1
        ....
        // command n
} while (condition);
```

Indu added the logic as shown below:

```
do {
        cin >> Tam;
        if(Tam <0 && Tam > 100)
                cout <<"\nEntered Tamil mark is incorrect";
}
while(Tam <0 && Tam > 100);
```

Bubesh said, "Good. The idea is to get a mark, check it, display an error for an invalid value, and repeat until a valid value is entered."

Harsha pointed out another improvement. "The prompt should also be inside the loop. Otherwise, when the loop repeats, the user will be expected to type another mark without being prompted again."

Thea said, "Beginners often make this kind of mistake, and experience gradually teaches us to notice it earlier. It is encouraging that you are already identifying such issues as a team. This kind of shared thinking is one of the strengths of teamwork. You are doing a good job—keep it up."

Indu updated the code:

```
do {
        cout << "\nEnter Tamil mark :";
        cin >> Tam;
        if(Tam <0 && Tam > 100)
                cout <<"\nEntered Tamil mark is incorrect";
}
while(Tam <0 && Tam > 100);
```

Bubesh agreed and suggested applying the same pattern to the other subjects. Indu extended the code accordingly.

```
do {
        cout << "\nEnter English mark :";
        cin >> Eng;
        if(Eng <0 && Eng > 100)
                cout <<"\nEntered English mark is incorrect";
}
while(Eng <0 && Eng > 100);
```

```
do {
        cout << "\nEnter Maths mark :";
        cin >> Mat;
        if(Mat <0 && Mat > 100)
                cout <<"\nEntered Maths mark is incorrect";
}
while(Mat <0 && Mat > 100);

do {
        cout << "\nEnter Science mark :";
        cin >> Sci;
        if(Sci <0 && Sci > 100)
                cout <<"\nEntered Science mark is incorrect";
}
while(Sci <0 && Sci > 100);

do {
        cout << "\nEnter Social mark :";
        cin >> Soc;
        if(Soc <0 && Soc > 100)
                cout <<"\nEntered Social mark is incorrect";
}
while(Soc <0 && Soc > 100);
```

Bubesh agreed to compile the updated program. The complete version at this stage is shown below:

```
#include "stdafx.h"
#include <iostream>

using namespace std;

int _tmain(int argc, _TCHAR* argv[])
{
        int Tam, Eng, Mat, Sci, Soc, Tot;
        float Avg;

        cout<<"W E L C O M E, ALL THE BEST for your Learning of C";

        do {
                cout << "\nEnter Tamil mark :";
                cin >> Tam;
                if(Tam <0 && Tam > 100)
                        cout <<"\nEntered Tamil mark is incorrect";
        }
        while(Tam <0 && Tam > 100);

        do {
                cout << "\nEnter English mark :";
                cin >> Eng;
                if(Eng <0 && Eng > 100)
                        cout <<"\nEntered English mark is incorrect";
        }
        while(Eng <0 && Eng > 100);

        do {
                cout << "\nEnter Maths mark :";
                cin >> Mat;
                if(Mat <0 && Mat > 100)
                        cout <<"\nEntered Maths mark is incorrect";
        }
        while(Mat <0 && Mat > 100);

        do {
                cout << "\nEnter Science mark :";
                cin >> Sci;
```

```
            if(Sci <0 && Sci > 100)
                cout <<"\nEntered Science mark is incorrect";
        }
        while(Sci <0 && Sci > 100);

        do {
            cout << "\nEnter Social mark :";
            cin >> Soc;
            if(Soc <0 && Soc > 100)
                cout <<"\nEntered Social mark is incorrect";
        }
        while(Soc <0 && Soc > 100);
        Tot = Tam + Eng + Mat + Sci + Soc;

        Avg = Tot / 5.0;

        cout << "\nTamil :" << Tam;
        cout << "\nEnglish :" << Eng;
        cout << "\nMaths :" << Mat;
        cout << "\nScience :" << Sci;
        cout << "\nSocial :" << Soc;

        cout << "\nTotal :" << Tot;
        cout << "\nAverage : " << Avg;

        return 0;
}
```

Harsha ran the program and tested it with deliberately invalid marks.

```
W E L C O M E, ALL THE BEST for your Learning of C
Enter Tamil mark :190
Enter English mark :190
Enter Maths mark :190
Enter Science mark :190
Enter Social mark :190
Tamil :190
English :190
Maths :190
Science :190
Social :190
Total :950
Average : 190
```

To their surprise, the program accepted the invalid marks. The validation logic had failed.

Indu asked Harsha to try a mixture of valid and invalid values as well.

```
W E L C O M E, ALL THE BEST for your Learning of C
Enter Tamil mark :89
Enter English mark :67
Enter Maths mark :89
Enter Science mark :190
Enter Social mark :70
Tamil :89
English :67
Maths :89
Science :190
Social :70
Total :505
Average : 101
```

"What happened? The earlier parts were working," Harsha said.

They isolated the Tamil-mark validation and examined it carefully.

```
        do {
```

```
            cout << "\nEnter Tamil mark :";
            cin >> Tam;
            if(Tam <0 && Tam > 100)
                    cout <<"\nEntered Tamil mark is incorrect";
    }
    while(Tam <0 && Tam > 100);
```

They realized that the condition was incorrect. A mark is invalid if it is below 0 **or** above 100, but the program used the AND operator (`&&`). That condition would require the same value to be below 0 and above 100 at the same time, which is impossible. Therefore, the OR operator (`||`) should be used instead.

The same incorrect condition was also used in the `while` test. Because that condition could never become true, the loop ended after the first entry instead of asking again.

After discussing the logic, they corrected the condition as shown below:

```
do {
            cout << "\nEnter Tamil mark :";
            cin >> Tam;
            if(Tam <0 || Tam > 100)
                    cout <<"\nEntered Tamil mark is incorrect";
}
while(Tam <0 || Tam > 100);
```

“Let us not change every subject immediately,” Indu suggested. “First, we will correct and test one subject. Once we know the logic works, we can apply the same change to the others.”

Indu compiled the program and asked Harsha to test the corrected Tamil-mark logic.

```
W E L C O M E, ALL THE BEST for your Learning of C
Enter Tamil mark :190
Entered Tamil mark is incorrect
Enter Tamil mark :-1
Entered Tamil mark is incorrect
Enter Tamil mark :89
Enter English mark :
```

The validation now worked correctly for Tamil. After confirming it with both below-zero and above-100 values, Indu applied the same correction to the other subjects and gave the updated program to Harsha for further testing.

Harsha continued testing the updated program.

```
W E L C O M E, ALL THE BEST for your Learning of C
Enter Tamil mark :190
Entered Tamil mark is incorrect
Enter Tamil mark :-1
Entered Tamil mark is incorrect
Enter Tamil mark :89
Enter English mark :-1
Entered English mark is incorrect
Enter English mark :181
Entered English mark is incorrect
Enter English mark :76
Enter Maths mark :-15
Entered Maths mark is incorrect
Enter Maths mark :156
Entered Maths mark is incorrect
Enter Maths mark :100
Enter Science mark :-56
Entered Science mark is incorrect
Enter Science mark :145
Entered Science mark is incorrect
Enter Science mark :95
Enter Social mark :96
Entered Social mark is incorrect
```

```
Tamil :89
English :76
Maths :100
Science :95
Social :96
Total :456
Average : 91.2
```

Harsha was satisfied with the validation. For Social Science he had entered a valid mark directly, so that subject also passed the positive test. The input-validation checkpoint was now complete.

```
#include "stdafx.h"
#include <iostream>

using namespace std;

int _tmain(int argc, _TCHAR* argv[])
{
	int Tam, Eng, Mat, Sci, Soc, Tot;
	float Avg;
	char Res[5], Grd[3];

	cout<<"W E L C O M E, ALL THE BEST for your Learning of C";

	do {
		cout << "\nEnter Tamil mark :";
		cin >> Tam;
		if(Tam <0 || Tam > 100)
			cout <<"\nEntered Tamil mark is incorrect";
	}
	while(Tam <0 || Tam > 100);

	do {
		cout << "\nEnter English mark :";
		cin >> Eng;
		if(Eng <0 || Eng > 100)
			cout <<"\nEntered English mark is incorrect";
	}
	while(Eng < 0 || Eng > 100);

	do {
		cout << "\nEnter Maths mark :";
		cin >> Mat;
		if(Mat <0 || Mat > 100)
			cout <<"\nEntered Maths mark is incorrect";
	}
	while(Mat < 0 || Mat > 100);

	do {
		cout << "\nEnter Science mark :";
		cin >> Sci;
		if(Sci <0 || Sci > 100)
			cout <<"\nEntered Science mark is incorrect";
	}
	while(Sci < 0 || Sci > 100);

	do {
		cout << "\nEnter Social mark :";
		cin >> Soc;
		if(Soc <0 || Soc > 100)
			cout <<"\nEntered Social mark is incorrect";
	}
	while(Soc < 0 || Soc > 100);

	Tot = Tam + Eng + Mat + Sci + Soc;
```

```
        Avg = Tot / 5.0;

        cout << "\nTamil :" << Tam;
        cout << "\nEnglish :" << Eng;
        cout << "\nMaths :" << Mat;
        cout << "\nScience :" << Sci;
        cout << "\nSocial :" << Soc;

        cout << "\nTotal :" << Tot;
        cout << "\nAverage : " << Avg;

        int i;
        cin >> i;
        return 0;
}
```

LEARNING STEP — REPLACING REPETITION WITH A FUNCTION

Thea said, “The validation now meets the requirement, but notice how the same group of statements is repeated for every subject. Can we move that repeated work into one reusable code?”

Indu replied, “I think we can write a function and call it whenever we need a mark. Is that what you mean?”

Bubesh replied, “Yes. That should reduce the repeated code.”

Indu said, “I understand functions, but I have not used one like this before.”

Bubesh replied, “Let us try it together.”

Thea said, “Good. But this function has one additional challenge: the same function must work for different subjects. Try the simple version first; the limitation will become clear.” Bubesh wrote the first version of the function:

```
int getmark()
{
        int mark;
        do{
                cout<<"enter the mark : ";
                cin >> mark;
                if (mark<0 || mark>100 )
                        cout <<" \n Entered mark is invalid \n" ;
        } while (mark<0 || mark>100);

        return mark;
}
```

Harsha observed, “The function can get and validate a mark, but the prompt no longer tells us which subject we are entering.”

“Yes,” Indu agreed. “We need to pass the subject name to the function.”

Thea said, “Exactly. A function can receive information through parameters. Pass the subject name when you call it, and use that parameter while displaying the prompt.”

Indu updated the function to accept the subject name and showed one function call:

IDE NOTE — In this Visual Studio C++ environment, string literals such as "Tamil" are better treated as read-only. A later publication pass will standardize this parameter as `const char*` (and its prototype accordingly) without changing the learning objective of the example.

```
int getmark(char* sub)
{
        int mark;
        do{
                cout<<"enter the mark " << sub << " : ";
                cin >> mark;
                if (mark<0 || mark>100 )
                        cout <<" \n Entered " << sub << " mark is invalid \n" ;
        } while (mark<0 || mark>100);

        return mark;
}

Tam = getmark("Tamil");
```

"Yes, this should meet the requirement," all three agreed.

Indu applied the function to the program:

```
#include "stdafx.h"
#include <iostream>

using namespace std;

int _tmain(int argc, _TCHAR* argv[])
{
        int Tam, Eng, Mat, Sci, Soc, Tot;
        float Avg;
        char Res[5], Grd[3];

        cout<<"W E L C O M E, ALL THE BEST for your Learning of C";

        Tam = getmark("Tamil");
        Eng = getmark("English");
        Mat = getmark("Maths");
        Sci = getmark("Science");
        Soc = getmark("Social");
        Tot = Tam + Eng + Mat + Sci + Soc;

        Avg = Tot / 5.0;

        cout << "\nTamil :" << Tam;
        cout << "\nEnglish :" << Eng;
        cout << "\nMaths :" << Mat;
        cout << "\nScience :" << Sci;
        cout << "\nSocial :" << Soc;

        cout << "\nTotal :" << Tot;
        cout << "\nAverage : " << Avg;

        int i;
        cin >> i;
        return 0;
}
```

```
int getmark(char* sub)
{
	int mark;
	do{
		cout<<"enter the mark " << sub << " : ";
		cin >> mark;
		if (mark<0 || mark>100 )
			cout <<" \n Entered " << sub << " mark is invalid \n" ;
	} while (mark<0 || mark>100);

	return mark;
}
```

MISTAKE → COMPILER ERROR → FUNCTION PROTOTYPE
Thea cautioned, “This version may produce a compilation error. Go ahead and compile it; the error itself will help us understand another important concept.”

As Thea expected, the compiler reported the following error:

```
error C3861: 'getmark': identifier not found
```

Functions, Parameters and Prototypes

Thea explained, “`getmark()` is defined after the main function, but it is called before the compiler has seen a declaration for it. At the point of the call, the compiler does not yet know the function’s name, parameters or return type.”

Harsha asked, “Can we move the complete `getmark()` function above the main function?”

“Yes,” Thea replied. “That is one option. Another is to place a function prototype before the main function. The prototype tells the compiler the function name, the type of value it returns and the types of parameters it accepts. The complete function definition can then appear later.”

“What exactly is a prototype?” Indu asked.

Thea explained, “A prototype is a declaration of the function interface. In our example, `int` says the function returns an integer, `getmark` is the function name, and `char*` describes the input parameter type. The compiler can then check a call to the function before it reaches the full definition.”

She showed the prototype:

```
int getmark(char*);
```

Indu added the prototype and showed the complete program:

```
#include "stdafx.h"
#include <iostream>

using namespace std;

int getmark(char*);
```

```
int _tmain(int argc, _TCHAR* argv[])
{
        int Tam, Eng, Mat, Sci, Soc, Tot;
        float Avg;
        char Res[5], Grd[3];

        cout<<"W E L C O M E, ALL THE BEST for your Learning of C";

        Tam = getmark("Tamil");
        Eng = getmark("English");
        Mat = getmark("Maths");
        Sci = getmark("Science");
        Soc = getmark("Social");
        Tot = Tam + Eng + Mat + Sci + Soc;

        Avg = Tot / 5.0;

        cout << "\nTamil :" << Tam;
        cout << "\nEnglish :" << Eng;
        cout << "\nMaths :" << Mat;
        cout << "\nScience :" << Sci;
        cout << "\nSocial :" << Soc;

        cout << "\nTotal :" << Tot;
        cout << "\nAverage : " << Avg;

        int i;
        cin >> i;
        return 0;
}

int getmark(char* sub)
{
    int mark;
    do{
        cout<<"enter the mark " << sub << " : ";
        cin >> mark;
        if (mark<0 || mark>100 )
            cout <<" \n Entered " << sub << " mark is invalid \n" ;
    } while (mark<0 || mark>100);

    return mark;
}
```

She compiled the program successfully and gave it to Harsha for testing.

Harsha ran the positive test case and obtained the following result:

```
W E L C O M E, ALL THE BEST for your Learning of Center the mark Tamil : 89
enter the mark English : 76
enter the mark Maths : 100
enter the mark Science : 96
enter the mark Social : 95

Tamil :89
English :76
Maths :100
Science :96
Social :95
Total :456
Average : 91.2
```

He also tested the function with invalid values:

```
W E L C O M E, ALL THE BEST for your Learning of Center the mark Tamil : 190
Entered Tamil mark is invalid
enter the mark Tamil : 89
enter the mark English : 760
 Entered English mark is invalid
enter the mark English : 76
enter the mark Maths : 101
 Entered Maths mark is invalid
enter the mark Maths : 100
enter the mark Science : -1
 Entered Science mark is invalid
enter the mark Science : 96
enter the mark Social : -10
 Entered Social mark is invalid
enter the mark Social : 95
Tamil :89
English :76
Maths :100
Science :96
Social :95
Total :456
Average : 91.2
```

Harsha said, “I found two small presentation issues. The first Tamil prompt begins on the same line as the welcome message, and the word ‘enter’ is not capitalized consistently.”

Indu replied, “I noticed them too. I will correct the formatting.”

LEARNING STEP — RESULT AND GRADE

Bubesh said, “The input part looks good now. Next we need to determine the student’s RESULT and GRADE.”

They identified two decisions: first, determine whether the student has passed every subject; second, if the student has passed, determine the grade from the average.

```
if( Tam>=40 && Eng >= 40 && Mat >= 40 && Sci >= 40 && Soc >= 40)
{
		// It means all suject is pass
		// If grade is applicable only who pass it.
		// So use finding grade logic within this loop.

}
```

They first considered the two possible branches of the result decision: PASS when every subject meets the minimum mark and FAIL otherwise.

```
if( Tam>=40 && Eng >= 40 && Mat >= 40 && Sci >= 40 && Soc >= 40)
{
	cout << "\n\t Candidate is PASS ";

	if ( Avg >= 90.0)
		cout << " \n\t Candidate is A+ ";
	if ( Avg >= 80)
		cout << " \n\t Candidate is A2 ";
	if ( Avg >= 70)
		cout << " \n\t Candidate is B1 ";
	if ( Avg >= 60)
		cout << " \n\t Candidate is B2 ";
	if ( Avg >= 50)
		cout << " \n\t Candidate is C1 ";
	if ( Avg >= 40)
		cout << " \n\t Candidate is C2 ";
```

```
                if ( Avg >= 40)
                        cout << "\n\t Candidate is fail";


        }
```

```
If( condition) {
        // command 1.1
                ....
        // command 1.1n
}
Else {
        // command 2.1
                ....
        // command 2.n
}
```

Harsha said, “For the grade, we should use an `if ... else if` chain. Once one grade range matches, the remaining grade conditions should not also be evaluated as separate successful grades”.

```
If (condition#1)
{
        ///Success condition1
}
else if (condition#2)
{
        /// Success condition#2
}
```

Indu combined the PASS/FAIL decision with the grade-selection logic:

```
if( Tam>=40 && Eng >= 40 && Mat >= 40 && Sci >= 40 && Soc >= 40)
{
        cout << "\n\t Candidate is PASS ";

        if ( Avg >= 90.0)
                cout << " \n\t Candidate is A+ ";
        else if ( Avg >= 80)
                cout << " \n\t Candidate is A2 ";
        else if ( Avg >= 70)
                cout << " \n\t Candidate is B1 ";
        else if ( Avg >= 60)
                cout << " \n\t Candidate is B2 ";
        else if ( Avg >= 50)
                cout << " \n\t Candidate is C1 ";
        else if ( Avg >= 40)
                cout << " \n\t Candidate is C2 ";
}
else
{
  cout << "\n\t Candidate is fail";
}
```

They reviewed the logic together and expected it to meet the requirement.

The updated program was:

```
#include "stdafx.h"
#include <iostream>

using namespace std;
```

```
int getmark(char*);

int _tmain(int argc, _TCHAR* argv[])
{
        int Tam, Eng, Mat, Sci, Soc, Tot;
        float Avg;
        char Res[5], Grd[3];

        cout<<"W E L C O M E, ALL THE BEST for your Learning of C\n";

        Tam = getmark("Tamil");
        Eng = getmark("English");
        Mat = getmark("Maths");
        Sci = getmark("Science");
        Soc = getmark("Social");
        Tot = Tam + Eng + Mat + Sci + Soc;

        Avg = Tot / 5.0;

        cout << "\nTamil :" << Tam;
        cout << "\nEnglish :" << Eng;
        cout << "\nMaths :" << Mat;
        cout << "\nScience :" << Sci;
        cout << "\nSocial :" << Soc;

        cout << "\nTotal :" << Tot;
        cout << "\nAverage : " << Avg;

        if( Tam>=40 && Eng >= 40 && Mat >= 40 && Sci >= 40 && Soc >= 40)
        {
                cout << "\n\t Candidate is PASS ";

                if ( Avg >= 90.0)
                        cout << " \n\t Candidate is A+ ";
                else if ( Avg >= 80)
                        cout << " \n\t Candidate is A2 ";
                else if ( Avg >= 70)
                        cout << " \n\t Candidate is B1 ";
                else if ( Avg >= 60)
                        cout << " \n\t Candidate is B2 ";
                else if ( Avg >= 50)
                        cout << " \n\t Candidate is C1 ";
                else if ( Avg >= 40)
                        cout << " \n\t Candidate is C2 ";
        }
        else
        {
          cout << "\n\t Candidate is fail";
        }

        return 0;
}

int getmark(char* sub)
{
        int mark;
        do{
                cout<<"Enter the mark " << sub << " : ";
                cin >> mark;
                if (mark<0 || mark>100 )
                        cout <<" \n Entere        d " << sub << " mark is invalid \n" ;
        } while (mark<0 || mark>100);
        return mark;
```

}

Indu compiled the program and gave the executable to Harsha for testing and Harsha ran the first test case:

```
Test case#1:
W E L C O M E, ALL THE BEST for your Learning of C
Enter the mark Tamil : 89
Enter the mark English : 76
Enter the mark Maths : 100
Enter the mark Science : 96
Enter the mark Social : 95
Tamil :89
English :76
Maths :100
Science :96
Social :95
Total :456
Average : 91.2
        Candidate is PASS
        Candidate is A+
Test case #2:
W E L C O M E, ALL THE BEST for your Learning of C
Enter the mark Tamil : 90
Enter the mark English : 80
Enter the mark Maths : 30
Enter the mark Science : 90
Enter the mark Social : 95
Tamil :90
English :80
Maths :30
Science :90
Social :95
Total :385
Average : 77
Candidate is fail
```

Harsha said, “The logic meets the test cases. We only need to improve the alignment and presentation of the result.”

Indu asked Bubesh, “Does this meet the requirement from the user’s point of view?”

LEARNING STEP — FROM ONE STUDENT TO MANY

Repeating the Process for Many Students

Bubesh replied, “For one student, yes. But the teacher has many students. At present we must run the program again for every student. The program should ask how many students need to be processed and repeat the same steps that many times.”

“That is a useful improvement,” Harsha agreed.

Indu replied, “We can get the number of students as input and use a `for` loop to repeat the processing. This is exactly the kind of repeated task a loop is meant for.”

She updated the program:

```
#include "stdafx.h"
#include <iostream>

using namespace std;

int getmark(char*);
```

```
int _tmain(int argc, _TCHAR* argv[])
{
        int Tam, Eng, Mat, Sci, Soc, Tot;
        float Avg;
        int i,n;

        cout<<"W E L C O M E, ALL THE BEST for your Learning of C\n";

        cout << "\nHow many students need to be processed? : ";
        cin >> n;

        for(i=0; i<n; i++)
        {

                Tam = getmark("Tamil");
                Eng = getmark("English");
                Mat = getmark("Maths");
                Sci = getmark("Science");
                Soc = getmark("Social");
                Tot = Tam + Eng + Mat + Sci + Soc;

                Avg = Tot / 5.0;

                cout << "\nTamil :" << Tam;
                cout << "\nEnglish :" << Eng;
                cout << "\nMaths :" << Mat;
                cout << "\nScience :" << Sci;
                cout << "\nSocial :" << Soc;

                cout << "\nTotal :" << Tot;
                cout << "\nAverage : " << Avg;

                if( Tam>=40 && Eng >= 40 && Mat >= 40 && Sci >= 40 && Soc >= 40)
                {
                        cout << "\n\t Candidate is PASS ";

                        if ( Avg >= 90.0)
                                cout << " \n\t Candidate is A+ ";
                        else if ( Avg >= 80)
                                cout << " \n\t Candidate is A2 ";
                        else if ( Avg >= 70)
                                cout << " \n\t Candidate is B1 ";
                        else if ( Avg >= 60)
                                cout << " \n\t Candidate is B2 ";
                        else if ( Avg >= 50)
                                cout << " \n\t Candidate is C1 ";
                        else if ( Avg >= 40)
                                cout << " \n\t Candidate is C2 ";
                }
                else
                {
                  cout << "\n\t Candidate is fail";
                }
        }

        return 0;
}

int getmark(char* sub)
{
        int mark;
        do{
```

```
            cout<<"Enter the mark " << sub << " : ";
            cin >> mark;
            if (mark<0 || mark>100 )
                cout <<" \n Entered " << sub << " mark is invalid \n" ;
    } while (mark<0 || mark>100);

    return mark;
}
```

Indu compiled the program and handed it to Harsha for testing.

Harsha tested it with three students. The output is shown below:

```
W E L C O M E, ALL THE BEST for your Learning of C
How many students mark to be processed? : 3
Enter the mark Tamil : 89
Enter the mark English : 76
Enter the mark Maths : 100
Enter the mark Science : 96
Enter the mark Social : 95
Tamil :89
English :76
Maths :100
Science :96
Social :95
Total :456
Average : 91.2
Candidate is PASS
Candidate is A+
Enter the mark Tamil : 50
Enter the mark English : 60
Enter the mark Maths : 70
Enter the mark Science : 50
Enter the mark Social : 60
Tamil :50
English :60
Maths :70
Science :50
Social :60
Total :290
Average : 58
Candidate is PASS
Candidate is C1
Enter the mark Tamil : 90
Enter the mark English : 60
Enter the mark Maths : 70
Enter the mark Science : 20
Enter the mark Social : 90
Tamil :90
English :60
Maths :70
Science :20
Social :90
Total :330
Average : 66
Candidate is fail
```

Harsha accepted the test results, and he will continue with more testing.

Thea also felt good and congratulated to complete the needs. Harsha and Indu agreed to show the program with RC and CK sir. But Bubesh compared the situation with existing processes to look for the benefits.

This program runs, needs to provide input, so it will calculate, average the mark, and it will tell the grade. In existing case, sir used to do add marks and divide by number of subjects. In this case, I need to run the program every time, so not seen big differences, or in other way this program is not fully reduced work for our class teacher. For the next person I must run the program again. Why do we need for every student?"

Harsha added, "Right, I think this can be easily modified with looping it based on number students".

Indu, "Got you, it can be managed with simple looping. This time we knew how many students in our class, so we can loop that many times and reduce the rerun the program. I am using for() loop for this purpose".

Harsha explained loop structure

```
for( initiation; condition; incremental)
{
        // statement 1
        // statement 2
        ---
        // statement n
}
```

"In our class we do have 50 students, so I will structure the command as follows", Indu worded and coded.

```
for(int i=0; i<50; i++)
{
        //bring all statements within this loop
}
```

Indu explained her understanding: "The program initializes `i` to 0 and increases it by one after each iteration. The statements inside the braces continue to run while `i` is less than 50. When `i` reaches 50, the condition `i=50 < 50` becomes false, so the loop ends."

Harsha added, "That works for our class of 50 students, but other classes may have a different number. During testing, I may also want to try the program with only a few students. If we accept the number of students as input, testing will be easier and the same program can be used for other classes without changing the code. Am I correct?"

Indu, "Yes, you are absolutely correct, I will get input and modify program accordingly".

```
#include "stdafx.h"
        #include <iostream>

        using namespace std;

        int getmark(char*);

        int _tmain(int argc, _TCHAR* argv[])
        {
                int Tam, Eng, Mat, Sci, Soc, Tot;
                float Avg;
                char Res[5], Grd[3];
                int i,n;

                cout<<"W E L C O M E, ALL THE BEST for your Learning of C\n";
```

```
        cout << "\nHow many students need to be processed? : ";
        cin >> n;

        for(i=0; i<n; i++)
        {

                Tam = getmark("Tamil");
                Eng = getmark("English");
                Mat = getmark("Maths");
                Sci = getmark("Science");
                Soc = getmark("Social");
                Tot = Tam + Eng + Mat + Sci + Soc;

                Avg = Tot / 5.0;

                cout << "\nTamil :" << Tam;
                cout << "\nEnglish :" << Eng;
                cout << "\nMaths :" << Mat;
                cout << "\nScience :" << Sci;
                cout << "\nSocial :" << Soc;

                cout << "\nTotal :" << Tot;
                cout << "\nAverage : " << Avg;

                if( Tam>=40 && Eng >= 40 && Mat >= 40 && Sci >= 40 && Soc >= 40)
                {
                        cout << "\nCandidate is PASS ";

                        if ( Avg >= 90.0)
                                cout << "\nCandidate is A+ \n";
                        else if ( Avg >= 80)
                                cout << "\nCandidate is A2 \n";
                        else if ( Avg >= 70)
                                cout << "\nCandidate is B1 \n";
                        else if ( Avg >= 60)
                                cout << "\nCandidate is B2 \n";
                        else if ( Avg >= 50)
                                cout << "\nCandidate is C1 \n";
                        else if ( Avg >= 40)
                                cout << "\nCandidate is C2 \n";
                }
                else
                {
                  cout << "\nCandidate is fail \n";
                }
        }

        cin >> i;
        return 0;
    }

int getmark(char* sub)
{
    int mark;
    do{
        cout<<"Enter the mark " << sub << " : ";
        cin >> mark;
        if (mark<0 || mark>100 )
                cout <<" \n Entered " << sub << " mark is invalid \n" ;
    } while (mark<0 || mark>100);

    return mark;
}
```

Harsha executed program and showed the results

```
W E L C O M E, ALL THE BEST for your Learning of C
How many students mark to be processed? : 2
Enter the mark Tamil : 90
Enter the mark English : 90
Enter the mark Maths : 50
Enter the mark Science : 50
Enter the mark Social : 90
Tamil :90
English :90
Maths :50
Science :50
Social :90
Total :370
Average : 74
Candidate is PASS
Candidate is B1
Enter the mark Tamil : 80
Enter the mark English : 60
Enter the mark Maths : 120
Entered Maths mark is invalid
Enter the mark Maths : 20
Enter the mark Science : 90
Enter the mark Social : 90
Tamil :80
English :60
Maths :20
Science :90
Social :90
Total :340
Average : 68
Candidate is fail
```

"Looks fine, but when I enter only two marks, it may be easy, when more marks, I don't know how many mark so far, we processed. If you add appropriate status or ask with such details, it will be good. Also, when we process, demarcation should be done by some line between the students. Please add it", Harsha added his comments after tested it.

Indu modified the program as shown below, she added, "Only differentiated the major changes, there are some cosmetic changes also done in the program, it is you have to compare between the last results and this results and find the right one".

```
#include "stdafx.h"
#include <iostream>

using namespace std;

int getmark(char*);

int _tmain(int argc, _TCHAR* argv[])
{
        int Tam, Eng, Mat, Sci, Soc, Tot;
        float Avg;
        char Res[5], Grd[3];
        int i,n;

        cout<<"W E L C O M E, ALL THE BEST for your Learning of C\n";

        cout << "\nHow many students need to be processed? : ";
        cin >> n;

        for(i=0; i<n; i++)
```

```
{
        cout << "\n######################################## : ";
        cout << "\n\tEnter the marks of student : " << i << "\n";
        Tam = getmark("Tamil");
        Eng = getmark("English");
        Mat = getmark("Maths");
        Sci = getmark("Science");
        Soc = getmark("Social");
        Tot = Tam + Eng + Mat + Sci + Soc;

        Avg = Tot / 5.0;

        cout << "\n\tTamil :" << Tam;
        cout << "\n\tEnglish :" << Eng;
        cout << "\n\tMaths :" << Mat;
        cout << "\n\tScience :" << Sci;
        cout << "\n\tSocial :" << Soc;

        cout << "\n\tTotal :" << Tot;
        cout << "\n\tAverage : " << Avg;

        if( Tam>=40 && Eng >= 40 && Mat >= 40 && Sci >= 40 && Soc >= 40)
        {
                cout << "\n\tCandidate is PASS ";

                if ( Avg >= 90.0)
                        cout << "\n\tCandidate is A+ \n";
                else if ( Avg >= 80)
                        cout << "\n\tCandidate is A2 \n";
                else if ( Avg >= 70)
                        cout << "\n\tCandidate is B1 \n";
                else if ( Avg >= 60)
                        cout << "\n\tCandidate is B2 \n";
                else if ( Avg >= 50)
                        cout << "\n\tCandidate is C1 \n";
                else if ( Avg >= 40)
                        cout << "\n\tCandidate is C2 \n";
        }
        else
        {
          cout << "\n\tCandidate is FAIL \n";
        }
}
cout << "\n################## MARK PROCESS END #######################";
cin >> i;
return 0;
}

int getmark(char* sub)
{
        int mark;
        do{
                cout<<"\tEnter the mark of " << sub << " : ";
                cin >> mark;
                if (mark<0 || mark>100 )
                        cout <<"\nEntered " << sub << " mark is invalid" ;
        } while (mark<0 || mark>100);

        return mark;
}
```

Harsha tested and showed results

```
How many students mark to be processed? : 2
##########################################:
    Enter the marks of student : 0
    Enter the mark of Tamil : 90
    Enter the mark of English : 90
    Enter the mark of Maths : 90
    Enter the mark of Science : 90
    Enter the mark of Social : 90
    Tamil :90
    English :90
    Maths :90
    Science :90
    Social :90
   Total :450
   Average : 90
   Candidate is PASS
   Candidate is A+
##########################################:
    Enter the marks of student : 1
    Enter the mark of Tamil : 50
    Enter the mark of English : 30
    Enter the mark of Maths : 99
    Enter the mark of Science : 99
    Enter the mark of Social : 99
    Tamil :50
    English :30
    Maths :99
    Science :99
    Social :99
   Total :377
   Average : 75.4
   Candidate is FAIL
################## MARK PROCESS END #######################
```

He was satisfied with the results. Bubesh also felt that the program was ready to be demonstrated to CK Sir and RC Sir. The students were excited and decided to meet the teachers at school the next day. Indu agreed to bring her laptop.

Bubesh arrived early and spoke with CK Sir and RC Sir to arrange a time for the demonstration. Both teachers were in the computer lab and were pleasantly surprised to hear that the students were already ready.

“Wow! That was quick. I did not expect you to be ready so soon,” CK Sir exclaimed.

RC Sir was encouraging but cautious. “Let us see how well they have built it,” he said. They agreed to meet during the morning tea break.

Agreed to meet during morning tea break.

When Bubesh shared the news, Indu and Harsha became a little nervous. They decided to run one more round of tests. The results were satisfactory, but their excitement and nervousness remained.

They met in the computer lab. Indu tried to log in to the laptop, but entered the password incorrectly.

Harsha tried again and successfully opened the laptop. CK Sir could see that they were nervous, perhaps because this was their first formal demonstration.

CK Sir asked students to sit comfortably and gave chocolates.

Indu replied, “Sir, we will have chocolates after demo and if you feel the program is useful”.

CK Sir replied, “The chocolates are not a reward for the program. You made a sincere effort to solve a real problem and help me. That effort itself deserves appreciation, so please have them.”

His words reassured them, and they had chocolates. They were still excited, but they now felt more comfortable.

RC sir gave an introduction, “This program is helping you to calculate student marks, find average and give a grade with following interactions”.

Step 1: The program asks how many students need to be processed for your class, and then collects and processes the marks for that number of students.

Step 2: For each student, it accepts all subject marks, calculates the TOTAL and AVERAGE, and determines the GRADE and RESULT.

CK Sir wants to run the program, before that he took the report of the completed month and used the same marks to compare exactly. This is bit different from test cases of Harsha, because he had some data that he put on his own. Here is original data processed in the last month, and it can be compared with existing report card. This process in Information technology called it **USER ACCEPTANCE TEST**.

So, program started and the results were shown below

```
W E L C O M E, ALL THE BEST for your Learning of C
How many students mark to be processed? : 5
########################################## :
    Enter the marks of student : 0
    Enter the mark of Tamil : 90
    Enter the mark of English : 67
    Enter the mark of Maths : 95
    Enter the mark of Science : 89
    Enter the mark of Social : 90
    Tamil :90
    English :67
    Maths :95
    Science :89
    Social :90
   Total :431
   Average : 86.2
   Candidate is PASS
   Candidate is A2
########################################## :
    Enter the marks of student : 1
    Enter the mark of Tamil : 56
    Enter the mark of English : 40
    Enter the mark of Maths : 90
    Enter the mark of Science : 70
    Enter the mark of Social : 60
    Tamil :56
    English :40
    Maths :90
    Science :70
    Social :60
    Total :316
    Average : 63.2
    Candidate is PASS
    Candidate is B2
########################################## :
    Enter the marks of student : 2
```

```
     Enter the mark of Tamil : 88
     Enter the mark of English : 78
     Enter the mark of Maths : 70
     Enter the mark of Science : 87
     Enter the mark of Social : 69
     Tamil :88
     English :78
     Maths :70
     Science :87
     Social :69
   Total :392
   Average : 78.4
   Candidate is PASS
   Candidate is B1
######################################## :
     Enter the marks of student : 3
     Enter the mark of Tamil : 60
     Enter the mark of English : 32
     Enter the mark of Maths : 56
     Enter the mark of Science : 44
     Enter the mark of Social : 57
     Tamil :60
     English :32
     Maths :56
     Science :44
     Social :57
   Total :249
   Average : 49.8
   Candidate is FAIL
######################################## :
     Enter the marks of student : 4
     Enter the mark of Tamil : 60
     Enter the mark of English : 70
     Enter the mark of Maths : 67
     Enter the mark of Science : 82
     Enter the mark of Social : 73
     Tamil :60
     English :70
     Maths :67
     Science :82
     Social :73
   Total :352
   Average : 70.4
   Candidate is PASS
   Candidate is B1
################## MARK PROCESS END ########################
```

CK Sir compared the results with his records. “The calculations are matching. But when we process several students, we also need a way to identify whose marks we are looking at. We should include the student’s name and, later, the roll number.”

RC Sir added, “This is the first phase. Next, you can store the students’ data, add ranking and produce a complete report in rank order.”

CK Sir replied, “Very good. Ranking also takes time when it is done manually. Give me the executable and I will continue testing it with more students and compare the results with my records.”

The students were happy with the demonstration and shared the executable program with CK Sir by email.

Bubesh asked, “Sir, what other features would make the program more useful?”

CK Sir replied, “I also prepare summary information for Headmaster Sriramulu Sir and the subject teachers. Can your program eventually generate information such as this?”

Total Number of students:
Total Students Passed and Percentage:
Total Failed Students and Percentage:
Total Students in each grade and Percentage:
Total Passed Students and failed students in each subject and class average mark of subject:

"Yes, sir. We can work towards that," all three replied confidently.

RC Sir smiled. "I can see that completing a working stage has increased your confidence.

That is one of the benefits of learning through a real problem."

All three replied together, "Thea helped us a lot."

RC Sir replied, "That is good. Her own project experience can help you. Also think about presenting the student results in a table; a well-organized report is easier to read and compare."

RC Sir continued, "You have reached a point where separate variables are becoming difficult to manage. Learn about arrays next. Arrays will let you store the same kind of data for many students under one variable name. Later, structures can help you group different pieces of information that belong to one student."

They thanked both teachers and left for class with excitement. They decided to meet again that evening.

Their next learning goal was clear: understand arrays.

PART V — DATA BECOMES INFORMATION

Arrays in Programming

They met again in the evening. Thea was there, and they excitedly described the day's demonstration. They thanked her for her support. Thea told them that helping them had also refreshed her own fundamentals and had been useful during the viva for her project.

She added, "That is one reason collaborative learning can be powerful. When you explain an idea to someone else, you often strengthen your own understanding too."

Thea began with the reason they needed arrays. "In the earlier version, the same variables were reused for each student. Once the next student's marks were entered, the previous values were no longer available in those variables. Before we solve that, let us distinguish data from information. If I simply say '56', what does that number tell you?"

Harsha replied, "It could be a subject mark."

Thea asked, "Which subject? Which student? You do not know. It could even represent an average or something completely different."

She continued, "A value such as 56 is data. When we add context—for example, 'the class average for Tamil in IX-D is 56'—the data becomes meaningful information. In simple terms, information is data interpreted in context."

"That makes it much clearer," Bubesh said.

Thea showed how awkward the program would become if they created a separate set of variables for every student:

```
int Tam1, Eng1, Mat1, Sci1, Soc1, Tot1;
float Avg1;
int Tam2, Eng2, Mat2, Sci2, Soc2, Tot2;
float Avg2;
int Tam3, Eng3, Mat3, Sci3, Soc3, Tot3;
float Avg3;
```

"For fifty students, this approach would require a very long list of variables and would be difficult to maintain. An array gives us a cleaner way to store many values of the same type under one name."

She rewrote the declarations using arrays:

```
int Tam[50], Eng[50], Mat[50], Sci[50], Soc[50], Tot[50];
float Avg[50];
```

"Now the student number can be represented by an index, which also works naturally with loops."

Harsha noticed the declarations for result and grade. "These are text values rather than single numbers. How do we store one result or grade for every student?"

Thea replied, "In this version we can use a two-dimensional `char` array. Think of it as a collection of character arrays: one small text buffer for each student."

```
char Res[50][5], Grd[50][3];
```

Arrays and Student Data

Indu added, “In `Tam[50]`, the array has space for fifty Tamil marks. C and C++ array indexing starts at 0, so `Tam[0]` is the first student’s mark and `Tam[5]` is the sixth student’s mark. In `Res[50][5]`, the first dimension represents students and the second provides character space for each student’s result text.”

Thea replied, “Arrays can have more dimensions when a problem genuinely needs them, but two dimensions are enough for what we are doing here.”

The three discussed the change and modified the program. At this stage they added storage for each student’s name so that the stored marks could be identified. They noted the roll number as a requirement to add in a later refinement.

```
#include "stdafx.h"
#include <iostream>

using namespace std;

int getmark(char*);

int _tmain(int argc, _TCHAR* argv[])
{
        int Tam[50], Eng[50], Mat[50], Sci[50], Soc[50], Tot[50];
        float Avg[50];
        char Res[50][5], Grd[50][3];
        int i,n;

        cout<<"W E L C O M E, ALL THE BEST for your Learning of C\n";

        cout << "\nHow many students need to be processed? : ";
        cin >> n;

        for(i=0; i<n; i++)
        {

                cout << "\n########################################## : ";
                cout << "\n\tEnter the marks of student : " << i << "\n";
                Tam[i] = getmark("Tamil");
                Eng[i] = getmark("English");
                Mat[i] = getmark("Maths");
                Sci[i] = getmark("Science");
                Soc[i] = getmark("Social");
                Tot[i] = Tam[i] + Eng[i] + Mat[i] + Sci[i] + Soc[i];

                Avg[i] = Tot[i] / 5.0;

                cout << "\n\tTamil :" << Tam[i];
                cout << "\n\tEnglish :" << Eng[i];
                cout << "\n\tMaths :" << Mat[i];
                cout << "\n\tScience :" << Sci[i];
                cout << "\n\tSocial :" << Soc[i];

                cout << "\n\tTotal :" << Tot[i];
                cout << "\n\tAverage : " << Avg[i] ;

                if( Tam[i]>=40 && Eng[i] >= 40 && Mat[i] >= 40 && Sci[i] >= 40 && Soc[i] >= 40)
                {
                        cout << "\n\tCandidate is PASS ";
```

```
                if ( Avg[i] >= 90.0)
                    cout << "\n\tCandidate is A+ \n";
                else if ( Avg[i] >= 80)
                    cout << "\n\tCandidate is A2 \n";
                else if ( Avg[i] >= 70)
                    cout << "\n\tCandidate is B1 \n";
                else if ( Avg[i] >= 60)
                    cout << "\n\tCandidate is B2 \n";
                else if ( Avg[i] >= 50)
                    cout << "\n\tCandidate is C1 \n";
                else if ( Avg[i] >= 40)
                    cout << "\n\tCandidate is C2 \n";
            }
            else
            {
              cout << "\n\tCandidate is FAIL \n";
            }
        }
        cout << "\n################## MARK PROCESS END ########################";
        cin >> i;
        return 0;
}

int getmark(char* sub)
{
        int mark;
        do{
                cout<<"\tEnter the mark of " << sub << " : ";
                cin >> mark;
                if (mark<0 || mark>100 )
                        cout <<"\nEntered " << sub << " mark is invalid" ;
        } while (mark<0 || mark>100);

        return mark;
}
```

The calculation logic was essentially the same, but the values were now stored in arrays. This meant the program could retain data for several students during the run. Harsha tested the revised version.

```
W E L C O M E, ALL THE BEST for your Learning of C
How many students mark to be processed? : 2
######################################## :
    Enter the marks of student : 0
    Enter the mark of Tamil : 90
    Enter the mark of English : 80
    Enter the mark of Maths : 100
    Enter the mark of Science : 88
    Enter the mark of Social : 93
    Tamil :90
    English :80
    Maths :100
    Science :88
    Social :93
   Total :451
   Average : 90.2
   Candidate is PASS
   Candidate is A+
######################################## :
    Enter the marks of student : 1
    Enter the mark of Tamil : 60
    Enter the mark of English : 33
    Enter the mark of Maths : 90
    Enter the mark of Science : 87
    Enter the mark of Social : 32
    Tamil :60
    English :33
```

```
    Maths :90
    Science :87
    Social :32
  Total :302
  Average : 60.4
  Candidate is FAIL
################### MARK PROCESS END ########################
```

Harsha observed, “Now that the marks are stored in the memory, we do not have to print each result immediately. Doing so would make my testing difficult as well. We can collect the inputs first and generate the report afterward. However, the stored data must be linked to a specific student identity.”

Indu agreed and added the student’s name to this stage of the program.

```
#include "stdafx.h"
#include <iostream>

using namespace std;

int getmark(char*);

int _tmain(int argc, _TCHAR* argv[])
{
        int Tam[50], Eng[50], Mat[50], Sci[50], Soc[50], Tot[50];
        float Avg[50];
        char Res[50][5], Grd[50][3], Nam[50][10];
        int i,n;

        cout<<"W E L C O M E, ALL THE BEST for your Learning of C\n";

        cout << "\nHow many students need to be processed? : ";
        cin >> n;

        for(i=0; i<n; i++)
        {

                cout << "\n######################################## : ";
                cout << "\n\tEnter the student Name[" << i << "]:";
                cin >> Nam[i];

                cout << "\n\tEnter the marks of " << Nam[i] << ":\n";
                Tam[i] = getmark("Tamil");
                Eng[i] = getmark("English");
                Mat[i] = getmark("Maths");
                Sci[i] = getmark("Science");
                Soc[i] = getmark("Social");
        }
        cout << "\n################### MARK INPUTS END ########################";

        // STUDENT MARK PROCESSED and REPORT GENERATED
        cout << "\n################### MARK REPORT BEGIN ########################";
        for(i=0; i<n; i++)
        {
                Tot[i] = Tam[i] + Eng[i] + Mat[i] + Sci[i] + Soc[i];

                Avg[i] = Tot[i] / 5.0;

                cout << "\n\tName :" << Nam[i];
                cout << "\n\tTamil :" << Tam[i];
                cout << "\n\tEnglish :" << Eng[i];
```

```
                    cout << "\n\tMaths :" << Mat[i];
                    cout << "\n\tScience :" << Sci[i];
                    cout << "\n\tSocial :" << Soc[i];

                    cout << "\n\tTotal :" << Tot[i];
                    cout << "\n\tAverage : " << Avg[i];

                    if( Tam[i]>=40 && Eng[i] >= 40 && Mat[i] >= 40 && Sci[i] >= 40 && Soc[i] >= 40)
                    {
                              cout << "\n\tCandidate is PASS ";

                              if ( Avg[i] >= 90.0)
                                        cout << "\n\tCandidate is A+ \n";
                              else if ( Avg[i] >= 80)
                                        cout << "\n\tCandidate is A2 \n";
                              else if ( Avg[i] >= 70)
                                        cout << "\n\tCandidate is B1 \n";
                              else if ( Avg[i] >= 60)
                                        cout << "\n\tCandidate is B2 \n";
                              else if ( Avg[i] >= 50)
                                        cout << "\n\tCandidate is C1 \n";
                              else if ( Avg[i] >= 40)
                                        cout << "\n\tCandidate is C2 \n";
                    }
                    else
                    {
                      cout << "\n\tCandidate is FAIL \n";
                    }
          }
          cout << "\n################## MARK REPORT END #######################";
          cin >> i;
          return 0;
}

int getmark(char* sub)
{
          int mark;
          do{
                    cout<<"\tEnter the mark of " << sub << " : ";
                    cin >> mark;
                    if (mark<0 || mark>100 )
                              cout <<"\nEntered " << sub << " mark is invalid" ;
          } while (mark<0 || mark>100);

          return mark;
}
```

Harsha ran the program and checked the results.

```
W E L C O M E, ALL THE BEST for your Learning of C
How many students mark to be processed? : 2
######################################## :
     Enter the student Name[0]:Raghu
     Enter the marks of Raghu:
     Enter the mark of Tamil : 90
     Enter the mark of English : 78
     Enter the mark of Maths : 96
     Enter the mark of Science : 93
     Enter the mark of Social : 92
######################################## :
     Enter the student Name[1]:Suku
     Enter the marks of Suku:
     Enter the mark of Tamil : 99
     Enter the mark of English : 94
     Enter the mark of Maths : 100
     Enter the mark of Science : 33
     Enter the mark of Social : 88
```

```
################## MARK INPUTS END #####################
################## MARK REPORT BEGIN ######################
    Name :Raghu
    Tamil :90
    English :78
    Maths :96
    Science :93
    Social :92
  Total :449
  Average : 89.8
  Candidate is PASS
  Candidate is A2
  Name :Suku
    Tamil :99
    English :94
    Maths :100
    Science :33
    Social :88
  Total :414
  Average : 82.8
  Candidate is FAIL
################## MARK REPORT END #####################
```

From Raw Data to a Readable Report

Harsha pointed out, “The calculations are correct, but RC Sir suggested a tabular report. Can we display the results in rows and columns? Also, CK Sir asked for total class reports for each subject.”

Indu agreed and first sketched the kind of table they wanted the program to produce.

```
W E L C O M E, ALL THE BEST for your Learning of C
How many students mark to be processed? : 4
######################################## :
     Enter the student Name[0]:Raghu
     Enter the marks of Raghu:
     Enter the mark of Tamil : 99
     Enter the mark of English : 88
     Enter the mark of Maths : 77
     Enter the mark of Science : 66
     Enter the mark of Social : 55
######################################## :
     Enter the student Name[1]:Senthil
     Enter the marks of Senthil:
     Enter the mark of Tamil : 88
     Enter the mark of English : 99
     Enter the mark of Maths : 100
     Enter the mark of Science : 66
     Enter the mark of Social : 55
######################################## :
     Enter the student Name[2]:Suku
     Enter the marks of Suku:
     Enter the mark of Tamil : 77
     Enter the mark of English : 99
     Enter the mark of Maths : 100
     Enter the mark of Science : 100
     Enter the mark of Social : 88
######################################## :
     Enter the student Name[3]:Muru
     Enter the marks of Muru:
     Enter the mark of Tamil : 66
     Enter the mark of English : 45
     Enter the mark of Maths : 81
     Enter the mark of Science : 79
     Enter the mark of Social : 33
```

```
#################### MARK INPUTS END #########################
##############################################MARK REPORT BEGIN
################################################
Name :      Tamil  English  Maths   Science  Social  Total  Average Result  Grade
Raghu        99      88      77       66       55     385     77     PASS    B1
Senthil      88      99     100       66       55     408     81.6   PASS    A2
Suku         77      99     100      100       88     464     92.8   PASS    A+
Muru         66      45      81       79       33     304     60.8   FAIL
############################################ MARK REPORT END
################################################
```

"The information is correct. We only need to improve the alignment and formatting," Harsha said.

Indu modified the output formatting and showed the updated program.

```
#include "stdafx.h"
#include <iostream>

using namespace std;

int getmark(char*);

int _tmain(int argc, _TCHAR* argv[])
{
        int Tam[50], Eng[50], Mat[50], Sci[50], Soc[50], Tot[50];
        float Avg[50];
        char Res[50][5], Grd[50][3], Nam[50][10];
        int i,n;

        cout<<"W E L C O M E, ALL THE BEST for your Learning of C\n";

        cout << "\nHow many students need to be processed? : ";
        cin >> n;

        for(i=0; i<n; i++)
        {

                cout << "\n########################################## : ";
                cout << "\n\tEnter the student Name[" << i << "]:";
                cin >> Nam[i];

                cout << "\n\tEnter the marks of " << Nam[i] << ":\n";
                Tam[i] = getmark("Tamil");
                Eng[i] = getmark("English");
                Mat[i] = getmark("Maths");
                Sci[i] = getmark("Science");
                Soc[i] = getmark("Social");
        }
        cout << "\n################## MARK INPUTS END ########################";

        // STUDENT MARK PROCESSED and REPORT GENERATED
        cout << "\n##########################################################MARK REPORT
BEGIN #########################################################################\n";
        cout << "\nName       \tTamil  English  Maths          Science  Social  Total  Average
Grade  Result\n";
        for(i=0; i<n; i++)
        {
                Tot[i] = Tam[i] + Eng[i] + Mat[i] + Sci[i] + Soc[i];

                Avg[i] = Tot[i] / 5.0;
```

```
cout <<"\n"<< Nam[i] <<"\t\t"<< Tam[i] <<"\t\t"<< Eng[i] <<"\t"<< Mat[i] <<"\t\t"<<
Sci[i] <<"\t\t"<< Soc[i] <<"\t\t"<< Tot[i] <<"\t\t"<< Avg[i];

        if( Tam[i]>=40 && Eng[i] >= 40 && Mat[i] >= 40 && Sci[i] >= 40 && Soc[i] >= 40)
        {
                cout << "\t\tPASS ";

                if ( Avg[i] >= 90.0)
                        cout << "\tA+";
                else if ( Avg[i] >= 80)
                        cout << "\tA2";
                else if ( Avg[i] >= 70)
                        cout << "\tB1";
                else if ( Avg[i] >= 60)
                        cout << "\tB2";
                else if ( Avg[i] >= 50)
                        cout << "C1";
                else if ( Avg[i] >= 40)
                        cout << "\t--";
        }
        else
        {
          cout << "\tFAIL \n";
        }
    }
    cout << "\n####################################3################ MARK REPORT
END ################################################################";
    cin >> i;
    return 0;
}

int getmark(char* sub)
{
        int mark;
        do{
                cout<<"\tEnter the mark of " << sub << " : ";
                cin >> mark;
                if (mark<0 || mark>100 )
                        cout <<"\nEntered " << sub << " mark is invalid" ;
        } while (mark<0 || mark>100);

        return mark;
}
```

Harsha ran the program. The report was much easier to compare, although some column spacing still needed adjustment.

```
W E L C O M E, ALL THE BEST for your Learning of C
How many students mark to be processed? : 5
######################################## :
        Enter the student Name[0]:Sruthi
        Enter the marks of Sruthi:
        Enter the mark of Tamil : 88
        Enter the mark of English : 89
        Enter the mark of Maths : 100
        Enter the mark of Science : 80
        Enter the mark of Social : 70
######################################## :
        Enter the student Name[1]:Magathi
        Enter the marks of Magathi:
        Enter the mark of Tamil : 80
        Enter the mark of English : 90
        Enter the mark of Maths : 95
        Enter the mark of Science : 98
```

```
    Enter the mark of Social : 99
######################################## :
    Enter the student Name[2]:Hasini
    Enter the marks of Hasini:
    Enter the mark of Tamil : 90
    Enter the mark of English : 70
    Enter the mark of Maths : 50
    Enter the mark of Science : 100
    Enter the mark of Social : 90
######################################## :
    Enter the student Name[3]:Vikardhan
    Enter the marks of Vikardhan:
    Enter the mark of Tamil : 99
    Enter the mark of English : 70
    Enter the mark of Maths : 100
    Enter the mark of Science : 90
    Enter the mark of Social : 60
######################################## :
    Enter the student Name[4]:Balu
    Enter the marks of Balu:
    Enter the mark of Tamil : 100
    Enter the mark of English : 50
    Enter the mark of Maths : 100
    Enter the mark of Science : 90
    Enter the mark of Social : 33
################## MARK INPUTS END ########################
##########################################MARK REPORT BEGIN
##################################################
Name  Tamil  English  Maths  Science  Social  Total  Average  Grade  Result
Sruthi     88        89        100       80        70        427        85.4
PASS    A2
Magathi    80        90        95        98        99        462        92.4
PASS    A+
Hasini     90        70        50        100       90        400        80
PASS    A2
Vikardhan  99        70        100       90        60        419        83.8      PASS
        A2
Balu       100       50        100       90        33        373        74.6      FAIL

######################################### MARK REPORT END
###################################################
```

Harsha asked Indu to make one more formatting adjustment and run the program again.

```
W E L C O M E, ALL THE BEST for your Learning of C
How many students mark to be processed? : 2
######################################## :
    Enter the student Name[0]:Thea
    Enter the marks of Thea:
    Enter the mark of Tamil : 90100
Entered Tamil mark is invalid   Enter the mark of Tamil : 100
    Enter the mark of English : 100
    Enter the mark of Maths : 100
    Enter the mark of Science : 90
    Enter the mark of Social : 90
######################################## :
    Enter the student Name[1]:Indi
    Enter the marks of Indi:
    Enter the mark of Tamil : 100
    Enter the mark of English : 90
    Enter the mark of Maths : 90
    Enter the mark of Science : 90
```

```
    Enter the mark of Social : 100
################### MARK INPUTS END #########################
##########################################################MARK REPORT BEGIN
########################################################
Name  Tamil  English  Maths  Science  Social  Total  Average  Grade  Result
Thea        100              100       100      90        90       480      96       PASS    A+
Indi        100               90        90      90       100       470      94       PASS    A+
########################################################## MARK REPORT END
####################################################
```

All three agreed that the report was now readable enough to continue. The next requirement was ranking, which meant arranging students by total mark in descending order.

THINK BEFORE CODE — How can we rank students?

This was a different kind of problem. Before writing code, they needed to understand the sorting logic. They returned to what they had observed CK Sir doing manually: identify the highest total first, then the next highest, and continue until the students are arranged in order.

They used a small set of totals to understand the idea step by step.

```
420    490    490
390    390    444
490    420
444    444
393    393
```

They began by comparing 420 with 390. Since 420 was larger, their order did not need to change.

Next, they compared 420 with 490. Since 490 was larger, the values needed to exchange positions if the list was to be arranged from highest to lowest.

“Can we make the program perform these comparisons and exchanges automatically?” Harsha asked.

Indu replied, “Let us divide the program into four stages. First, collect the inputs. Second, calculate total, average, result and grade. Third, sort the students in descending order of total. Fourth, print the report in that order so that ranking becomes clear.”

Indu continued, “Before adding the sorting logic, I will restructure the existing program so that result and grade are stored rather than printed immediately. The behaviour will remain the same, but the data will then be available when we sort and print the final report”.

All agreed with the step-by-step approach.

Indu modified the program and showed the revised version.

```
#include "stdafx.h"
#include <iostream>

using namespace std;
```

```
int getmark(char*);

int _tmain(int argc, _TCHAR* argv[])
{
	int Tam[50], Eng[50], Mat[50], Sci[50], Soc[50], Tot[50];
	float Avg[50];
	char Res[50][5], Grd[50][4], Nam[50][10];
	int i,n;

	cout<<"W E L C O M E, ALL THE BEST for your Learning of C\n";

	cout << "\nHow many students need to be processed? : ";
	cin >> n;

	for(i=0; i<n; i++)
	{

		cout << "\n########################################## : ";
		cout << "\n\tEnter the student Name[" << i << "]:";
		cin >> Nam[i];

		cout << "\n\tEnter the marks of " << Nam[i] << ":\n";
		Tam[i] = getmark("Tamil");
		Eng[i] = getmark("English");
		Mat[i] = getmark("Maths");
		Sci[i] = getmark("Science");
		Soc[i] = getmark("Social");
	}
	cout << "\n################# MARK INPUTS END #####################";

	// STUDENT MARK CALCULATION PROCESS DONE HERE
	for(i=0; i<n; i++)
	{
		Tot[i] = Tam[i] + Eng[i] + Mat[i] + Sci[i] + Soc[i];

		Avg[i] = Tot[i] / 5.0;

		if( Tam[i]>=40 && Eng[i] >= 40 && Mat[i] >= 40 && Sci[i] >= 40 && Soc[i] >= 40)
		{
			strcpy(Res[i], "PASS"); //cout << "\tPASS ";

			if ( Avg[i] >= 90.0)
				strcpy(Grd[i], "A+"); // cout << "\tA+";
			else if ( Avg[i] >= 80)
				strcpy(Grd[i], "A2"); // cout << "\tA2";
			else if ( Avg[i] >= 70)
				strcpy(Grd[i], "B1"); // cout << "\tB1";
			else if ( Avg[i] >= 60)
				strcpy(Grd[i], "B2"); // cout << "\tB2";
			else if ( Avg[i] >= 50)
				strcpy(Grd[i], "C1"); // cout << "\tC1";
			else if ( Avg[i] >= 40)
				strcpy(Grd[i], "C2"); // cout << "\t--";
		}
		else
		{
		  strcpy(Res[i], "FAIL"); //cout << "\tFAIL \n";
		  strcpy(Grd[i], "--"); // cout << "\t--";

		}
	}
```

```
                              // STUDENT MARK REPORT IS GENERATED HERE
                              cout << "\n##########################################################MARK REPORT
BEGIN #########################################################################\n";
                              cout << "\nName        \tTamil  English  Maths Science Social  Total  Average  Grade  Result\n";
                              for(i=0; i<n; i++)
                              {
                                          cout <<"\n"<< Nam[i] <<"\t\t"<< Tam[i] <<"\t"<< Eng[i] <<"\t"<< Mat[i] <<"\t"<< Sci[i]
<<"\t"<< Soc[i] <<"\t"<< Tot[i] <<"\t"<< Avg[i] <<"\t"<< Grd[i] <<"\t"<< Res[i];
                              }

                              cout << "\n############################################################ MARK REPORT
END ########          ##############################################################";


                              cin >> i;
                              return 0;
                    }

          int getmark(char* sub)
          {
                    int mark;
                    do{
                              cout<<"\tEnter the mark of " << sub << " : ";
                              cin >> mark;
                              if (mark<0 || mark>100 )
                                        cout <<"\nEntered " << sub << " mark is invalid" ;
                    } while (mark<0 || mark>100);

                    return mark;
          }
```

It is quick test for Harsha to produce with two student marks and results.

```
W E L C O M E, ALL THE BEST for your Learning of C
How many students mark to be processed? : 2
######################################## :
      Enter the student Name[0]:Kousal
      Enter the marks of Kousal:
      Enter the mark of Tamil : 88
      Enter the mark of English : 92
      Enter the mark of Maths : 100
      Enter the mark of Science : 89
      Enter the mark of Social : 87
######################################## :
      Enter the student Name[1]:Katy
      Enter the marks of Katy:
      Enter the mark of Tamil : 80
      Enter the mark of English : 99
      Enter the mark of Maths : 23
      Enter the mark of Science : 100
      Enter the mark of Social : 100
################## MARK INPUTS END #######################
##################################################MARK REPORT BEGIN
##################################################
Name   Tamil  English  Maths  Science Social  Total  Average  Grade  Result
Kousal       88     92     100    89     87     456     91.2    A+      PASS
Katy         80     99      23   100    100     402     80.4    --      FAIL
######################################################## MARK REPORT END
################################################
```

Sorting Students for Ranking

Indu said, “Now I am going to add the section that sorts the students according to their total marks.”

```
// CProg01.cpp : Defines the entry point for the console application.
//

        #include "stdafx.h"
        #include <iostream>

        using namespace std;

        int getmark(char*);

        int _tmain(int argc, _TCHAR* argv[])
        {
                int Tam[50], Eng[50], Mat[50], Sci[50], Soc[50], Tot[50];
                float Avg[50];
                char Res[50][10], Grd[50][10], Nam[50][10];
                int i,n;

                cout<<"W E L C O M E, ALL THE BEST for your Learning of C\n";

                cout << "\nHow many students need to be processed? : ";
                cin >> n;

                for(i=0; i<n; i++)
                {

                        cout << "\n######################################## : ";
                        cout << "\n\tEnter the student Name[" << i << "]:";
                        cin >> Nam[i];

                        cout << "\n\tEnter the marks of " << Nam[i] << ":\n";
                        Tam[i] = getmark("Tamil");
                        Eng[i] = getmark("English");
                        Mat[i] = getmark("Maths");
                        Sci[i] = getmark("Science");
                        Soc[i] = getmark("Social");
                }
                cout << "\n################### MARK INPUTS END #######################";

                // STUDENT MARK CALCULATION PROCESS DONE HERE
                for(i=0; i<n; i++)
                {
                        Tot[i] = Tam[i] + Eng[i] + Mat[i] + Sci[i] + Soc[i];

                        Avg[i] = Tot[i] / 5.0;

                        if( Tam[i]>=40 && Eng[i] >= 40 && Mat[i] >= 40 && Sci[i] >= 40 && Soc[i] >= 40)
                        {
                                strcpy(Res[i], "PASS"); //cout << "\tPASS ";

                                if ( Avg[i] >= 90.0)
                                        strcpy(Grd[i], "A+"); // cout << "\tA+";
                                else if ( Avg[i] >= 80)
                                        strcpy(Grd[i], "A2"); // cout << "\tA2";
                                else if ( Avg[i] >= 70)
                                        strcpy(Grd[i], "B1"); // cout << "\tB1";
                                else if ( Avg[i] >= 60)
                                        strcpy(Grd[i], "B2"); // cout << "\tB2";
```

```
                else if ( Avg[i] >= 50)
                        strcpy(Grd[i], "C1"); // cout << "\tC1";
                else if ( Avg[i] >= 40)
                        strcpy(Grd[i], "C2"); // cout << "\t--";
        }
        else
        {
                strcpy(Res[i], "FAIL"); //cout << "\tFAIL \n";
                strcpy(Grd[i], "--"); // cout << "\t--";

        }
}

// SORTING STUDENTS IN DESCENDING ORDER BASED ON TOTAL MARK

int j, Tmp;
float Fmp;
char Str[15];
for(i=0; i<(n-1); i++)
for(j=i+1; j<n; j++)
{
// Compare two total marks and exchange the student data when required
        if( Tot[i] > Tot[j])
        {
                // Exchange Total Mark
                Tmp = Tot[i];
                Tot[i] = Tot[j];
                Tot[j] = Tmp;

                // Exchange Tamil Mark
                Tmp = Tam[i];
                Tam[i] = Tam[j];
                Tam[j] = Tmp;

                // Exchange English Mark
                Tmp = Eng[i];
                Eng[i] = Eng[j];
                Eng[j] = Tmp;

                // Exchange Maths Mark
                Tmp = Mat[i];
                Mat[i] = Mat[j];
                Mat[j] = Tmp;

                // Exchange Science Mark
                Tmp = Sci[i];
                Sci[i] = Sci[j];
                Sci[j] = Tmp;

                // Exchange Total Mark
                Tmp = Soc[i];
                Soc[i] = Soc[j];
                Soc[j] = Tmp;

                // Exchange Average Mark
                Fmp = Avg[i];
                Avg[i] = Avg[j];
                Avg[j] = Fmp;

                // Exchange the Name
```

```
                                        strcpy(Str, Nam[i]);
                                        strcpy(Nam[i], Nam[j]);
                                        strcpy(Nam[j], Str);
                                        // Exchange the Res
                                        strcpy(Str, Res[i]);
                                        strcpy(Res[i], Res[j]);
                                        strcpy(Res[j], Str);

                                        // Exchange the Grade
                                        strcpy(Str, Grd[i]);
                                        strcpy(Grd[i], Grd[j]);
                                        strcpy(Grd[j], Str);
                                }
                        }
                        // STUDENT MARK REPORT IS GENERATED HERE
                        cout << "\n##############################################################MARK REPORT
BEGIN ###############################################################\n";
                        cout << "\nName        \tTamil  English  Maths Science Social  Total  Average  Grade  Result\n";
                        for(i=0; i<n; i++)
                        {
                                cout <<"\n"<< Nam[i] <<"\t\t"<< Tam[i] <<"\t"<< Eng[i] <<"\t"<< Mat[i] <<"\t"<< Sci[i]
<<"\t"<< Soc[i] <<"\t"<< Tot[i] <<"\t"<< Avg[i] <<"\t"<< Grd[i] <<"\t"<< Res[i];
                        }

                        cout << "\n################################################################ MARK REPORT
END ########          ###################################################";

                        cin >> i;
                        return 0;
                }

        int getmark(char* sub)
        {
                int mark;
                do{
                        cout<<"\tEnter the mark of " << sub << " : ";
                        cin >> mark;
                        if (mark<0 || mark>100 )
                                cout <<"\nEntered " << sub << " mark is invalid" ;
                } while (mark<0 || mark>100);

                return mark;
        }
```

MISTAKE → TEST → DEBUG → LEARN

Harsha tested the program. The totals were sorted correctly, but in ascending order—the lowest total appeared first. Their requirement was the opposite: ranking needed the highest total first.

```
W E L C O M E, ALL THE BEST for your Learning of C
How many students need to be processed? : 4
######################################## :
    Enter the student Name[0]:Kousel
    Enter the marks of Kousel:
    Enter the mark of Tamil : 90
    Enter the mark of English : 90
    Enter the mark of Maths : 80
    Enter the mark of Science : 90
    Enter the mark of Social : 90
######################################## :
    Enter the student Name[1]:Indu
    Enter the marks of Indu:
```

```
    Enter the mark of Tamil : 80
    Enter the mark of English : 50
    Enter the mark of Maths : 100
    Enter the mark of Science : 100
    Enter the mark of Social : 100
######################################## :
    Enter the student Name[2]:Thea
    Enter the marks of Thea:
    Enter the mark of Tamil : 90
    Enter the mark of English : 100
    Enter the mark of Maths : 100
    Enter the mark of Science : 100
    Enter the mark of Social : 99
######################################## :
    Enter the student Name[3]:Teety
    Enter the marks of Teety:
    Enter the mark of Tamil : 80
    Enter the mark of English : 90
    Enter the mark of Maths : 80
    Enter the mark of Science : 100
    Enter the mark of Social : 100
################## MARK INPUTS END ########################
####################################################MARK REPORT BEGIN
####################################################
Name    Tamil  English  Maths  Science Social  Total  Average  Grade  Result
Indu      80      50     100     100     100    430     86      A2     PASS
Kousel    90      90      80      90      90    440     88      A2     PASS
Teety     80      90      80     100     100    450     90      A+     PASS
Thea      90     100     100     100      99    489     97.8    A+     PASS
######################################################### MARK REPORT END
####################################################
```

Indu examined the comparison logic and corrected it so that a student with a larger total would move ahead of a student with a smaller total, while also adjusting the report format.

```
W E L C O M E, ALL THE BEST for your Learning of C
How many students need to be processed? : 5
######################################## :
    Enter the student Name[0]:Kousel
    Enter the marks of Kousel:
    Enter the mark of Tamil : 70
    Enter the mark of English : 80
    Enter the mark of Maths : 70
    Enter the mark of Science : 90
    Enter the mark of Social : 98
######################################## :
    Enter the student Name[1]:Deety
    Enter the marks of Deety:
    Enter the mark of Tamil : 89
    Enter the mark of English : 90
    Enter the mark of Maths : 60
    Enter the mark of Science : 90
    Enter the mark of Social : 100
######################################## :
    Enter the student Name[2]:Sruthi
    Enter the marks of Sruthi:
    Enter the mark of Tamil : 88
    Enter the mark of English : 100
    Enter the mark of Maths : 100
    Enter the mark of Science : 100
    Enter the mark of Social : 80
######################################## :
    Enter the student Name[3]:Sailu
```

```
Enter the marks of Sailu:
Enter the mark of Tamil : 90
Enter the mark of English : 80
Enter the mark of Maths : 99
Enter the mark of Science : 89
Enter the mark of Social : 79
########################################## :
Enter the student Name[4]:Vikar
Enter the marks of Vikar:
Enter the mark of Tamil : 100
Enter the mark of English : 90
Enter the mark of Maths : 100
Enter the mark of Science : 90
Enter the mark of Social : 100
################## MARK INPUTS END ########################
##################################################MARK REPORT BEGIN
######################################################################
Name Tamil English Maths Science Social Total Average Grade Result
Vikar     100   90   100   90   100   480   96    A+   PASS
Sruthi     88  100   100  100    80   468   93.6  A+   PASS
Sailu      90   80    99   89    79   437   87.4  A2   PASS
Deety      89   90    60   90   100   429   85.8  A2   PASS
Kousel     70   80    70   90    98   408   81.6  A2   PASS
##################################################### MARK REPORT END ########
##########################################################
```

Harsha checked the result and confirmed that the students were now listed in descending order of total marks.

Class Totals, Averages and Pass Counts

Bubesh then asked, “Can we also show class-level information such as each subject’s total and average?”

Indu agreed. “Yes. We can calculate the subject totals and averages. We can also count how many students passed each subject and how many passed overall.”

They first added variables for the class-level totals and averages.

```
int TamTot, EngTot, MatTot, SciTot, SocTot, TotTot;
float Avg[50], TamAvg,EngAvg, MatAvg, SciAvg, SocAvg, TotAvg, nStd;

// STUDENT MARK CALCULATION PROCESS DONE HERE
        for(i=0; i<n; i++)
        {
                Tot[i] = Tam[i] + Eng[i] + Mat[i] + Sci[i] + Soc[i];

                Avg[i] = Tot[i] / 5.0;

                if( Tam[i]>=40 && Eng[i] >= 40 && Mat[i] >= 40 && Sci[i] >= 40 && Soc[i] >= 40)
                {
                        strcpy(Res[i], "PASS"); //cout << "\tPASS ";

                        if ( Avg[i] >= 90.0)
                                strcpy(Grd[i], "A+"); // cout << "\tA+";
                        else if ( Avg[i] >= 80)
                                strcpy(Grd[i], "A2"); // cout << "\tA2";
                        else if ( Avg[i] >= 70)
                                strcpy(Grd[i], "B1"); // cout << "\tB1";
                        else if ( Avg[i] >= 60)
                                strcpy(Grd[i], "B2"); // cout << "\tB2";
                        else if ( Avg[i] >= 50)
                                strcpy(Grd[i], "C1"); // cout << "\tC1";
```

```
            else if ( Avg[i] >= 40)
                strcpy(Grd[i], "C2"); // cout << "\t--";
        }
        else
        {
            strcpy(Res[i], "FAIL"); //cout << "\tFAIL \n";
            strcpy(Grd[i], "--"); // cout << "\t--";
        }

        // AGGREGATING CLASS LEVEL
        TamTot = TamTot+ Tam[i];
        EngTot = EngTot+ Eng[i];
        MatTot = MatTot+ Mat[i];
        SciTot = SciTot+ Sci[i];
        SocTot = SocTot+ Soc[i];
        TotTot = TotTot+ Tot[i];
    }

    // CALCULATING SUBJECT AVERAGE
        nStd = (float) n;
        TamAvg = TamTot / nStd;
        EngAvg = EngTot / nStd;
        MatAvg = MatTot / nStd;
        SciAvg = SciTot / nStd;
        SocAvg = SocTot / nStd;
        TotAvg = TotTot / nStd;
```

Compiler Warnings and Initialization

When Indu compiled the program, Visual Studio reported warnings about uninitialized total variables.

```
warning C4700: uninitialized local variable 'TamTot' used
warning C4700: uninitialized local variable 'EngTot' used
warning C4700: uninitialized local variable 'MatTot' used
warning C4700: uninitialized local variable 'SciTot' used
warning C4700: uninitialized local variable 'SocTot' used
warning C4700: uninitialized local variable 'TotTot' used
```

COMPILER WARNING → INITIALIZATION → CORRECTION

They examined the warning. The statement `TamTot = TamTot + Tam[i];` assumes that `TamTot` already contains a known starting value. But a local variable that has not been initialized may contain an indeterminate value, so using it in a calculation can produce an incorrect result.

```
TamTot = TamTot+ Tam[i];
```

They corrected the problem by initializing every class-total variable to zero before the accumulation began:

```
int TamTot=0, EngTot=0, MatTot=0, SciTot=0, SocTot=0, TotTot=0;
```

After initializing the totals, the program compiled successfully.

Harsha ran the program with marks for three students. The class totals and averages were now produced as expected.

```
W E L C O M E, ALL THE BEST for your Learning of C
How many students need to be processed? : 3
############################################ :
    Enter the student Name[0]:Anns
    Enter the marks of Anns:
    Enter the mark of Tamil : 90
    Enter the mark of English : 78
```

```
     Enter the mark of Maths : 69
     Enter the mark of Science : 90
     Enter the mark of Social : 96
######################################## :
     Enter the student Name[1]:Mayil
     Enter the marks of Mayil:
     Enter the mark of Tamil : 85
     Enter the mark of English : 76
     Enter the mark of Maths : 100
     Enter the mark of Science : 56
     Enter the mark of Social : 65
######################################## :
     Enter the student Name[2]:Paddu
     Enter the marks of Paddu:
     Enter the mark of Tamil : 56
     Enter the mark of English : 86
     Enter the mark of Maths : 78
     Enter the mark of Science : 44
     Enter the mark of Social : 100
################## MARK INPUTS END #######################
######################MARK REPORT BEGIN ##########################################
Name      Tamil English Maths Science Social Total Average Grade Result
Anns        90     78     69      90    96    423   84.6     A2  PASS
Mayil       85     76    100      56    65    382   76.4     B1  PASS
Paddu       56     86     78      44   100    364   72.8     B1  PASS
####################################################################################
###
Sub Tot     231   240   247   190   261   1169
Sub Ave     77.0  80.0  82.33 63.33 87.0  389.67
############################## MARK REPORT END##################################
```

Harsha said, “This looks good. I will run more tests to confirm that the calculations remain correct with different data.”

Indu replied, “Before the final testing, let us review the program with Thea. If she suggests any changes, we can apply them first.”

Indu sent the program to Thea. She said she would review it and join them shortly.

Requirement Review

Meanwhile, the three students compared the program against CK Sir’s requirements using a checklist.

Requirement Review Checklist

1. Get the number of students and their five subject marks — Completed
2. Calculate total, average, result and grade for every student — Completed
3. Sort students by total marks for ranking — Completed
4. Calculate each subject total and average — Completed
5. Calculate the number of students who passed each subject — Missing
6. Report all students’ marks in tabular form — Completed
7. Print all subject totals — Completed
8. Print all subject averages — Completed
9. Print the number of students who passed and failed overall — Missing

Indu said, “I will include the missing items together with any review comments from Thea. Shall we take a short tea break?”

After tea and snacks, Thea joined them by video call.

PART VI — BUILDING A BETTER APPLICATION

From Separate Arrays to a Student Structure

From Separate Arrays to a Student Structure

She began, “Look at the sorting code. Whenever two students exchange positions, you are separately exchanging the name, five subject marks, total, average, result and grade. The code works, but all those values actually belong to one student. A structure can group them together, making the program easier to understand and maintain.”

```
for(i=0; i<(n-1); i++)
for(j=i+1; j<n; j++)
{
        //Compare two total marks, if small than exchange it
        if( Tot[i] < Tot[j])
        {
                // Exchange Total Mark
                Tmp = Tot[i];
                Tot[i] = Tot[j];
                Tot[j] = Tmp;

                // Exchange Tamil Mark
                Tmp = Tam[i];
                Tam[i] = Tam[j];
                Tam[j] = Tmp;

                // Exchange English Mark
                Tmp = Eng[i];
                Eng[i] = Eng[j];
                Eng[j] = Tmp;

                // Exchange Maths Mark
                Tmp = Mat[i];
                Mat[i] = Mat[j];
                Mat[j] = Tmp;

                // Exchange Science Mark
                Tmp = Sci[i];
                Sci[i] = Sci[j];
                Sci[j] = Tmp;

                // Exchange Total Mark
                Tmp = Soc[i];
                Soc[i] = Soc[j];
                Soc[j] = Tmp;

                // Exchange Average Mark
                Fmp = Avg[i];
                Avg[i] = Avg[j];
                Avg[j] = Fmp;

                // Exchange the Name
                strcpy(Str, Nam[i]);
                strcpy(Nam[i], Nam[j]);
                strcpy(Nam[j], Str);
                // Exchange the Res
                strcpy(Str, Res[i]);
                strcpy(Res[i], Res[j]);
                strcpy(Res[j], Str);
```

```
                    // Exchange the Grade
                    strcpy(Str, Grd[i]);
                    strcpy(Grd[i], Grd[j]);
                    strcpy(Grd[j], Str);
                }
            }
```

Bubesh said, “That makes sense. If all the details of one student are kept together, we can exchange the whole student record instead of swapping every field separately.”

Indu began reorganizing the student data using a structure.

Until now, the program stored related student information in separate arrays:

```
int Tam[50], Eng[50], Mat[50], Sci[50], Soc[50], Tot[50];
int TamTot=0, EngTot=0, MatTot=0, SciTot=0, SocTot=0, TotTot=0;
float Avg[50], TamAvg,EngAvg, MatAvg, SciAvg, SocAvg, TotAvg, nStd;
char Res[50][10], Grd[50][10], Nam[50][10];
```

CONCEPT — A structure groups related values under one record type. Here, a student’s name, subject marks, total, average, result and grade can travel together as one STUDENT record. This becomes especially useful during sorting because the entire student record can be exchanged in one operation.

They redesigned the data using a structure:

```
struct STUDENT {
            char Nam;
            int Tam;
            int Eng;
            int Mat;
            int Sci;
            int Soc;
            int Tot;
            float Avg;
            char Res[10];
            char Grd[10];
};
STUDFNT Std[50];
```

Thea agreed with the structure. Indu began implementing the change, and Thea said she would review the updated version again.

```
#include "stdafx.h"
#include <iostream>

using namespace std;

int getmark(char*);

struct STUDENT {
            char Nam[10];
            int Tam;
            int Eng;
            int Mat;
            int Sci;
            int Soc;
```

```
				int Tot;
				float Avg;
				char Res[10];
				char Grd[10];
		};
		int _tmain(int argc, _TCHAR* argv[])
		{
			//int Tam[50], Eng[50], Mat[50], Sci[50], Soc[50], Tot[50];
			STUDENT Std[50];
			int TamTot=0, EngTot=0, MatTot=0, SciTot=0, SocTot=0, TotTot=0;
			float Avg[50], TamAvg,EngAvg, MatAvg, SciAvg, SocAvg, TotAvg,
nStd;

			int i,n;

			cout<<"W E L C O M E, ALL THE BEST for your Learning of C\n";

			cout << "\nHow many students need to be processed? : ";
			cin >> n;

			for(i=0; i<n; i++)
			{

				cout << "\n######################################## : ";
				cout << "\n\tEnter the student Name[" << i << "]:";
				cin >> Std[i].Nam;

				cout << "\n\tEnter the marks of " << Std[i].Nam << ":\n";
				Std[i].Tam = getmark("Tamil");
				Std[i].Eng = getmark("English");
				Std[i].Mat = getmark("Maths");
				Std[i].Sci = getmark("Science");
				Std[i].Soc = getmark("Social");
			}
			cout << "\n################## MARK INPUTS END ########################";

			// STUDENT MARK CALCULATION PROCESS DONE HERE
			for(i=0; i<n; i++)
			{
				Std[i].Tot = Std[i].Tam + Std[i].Eng + Std[i].Mat + Std[i].Sci +
Std[i].Soc;

				Std[i].Avg = Std[i].Tot / 5.0;

				if( Std[i].Tam>=40 && Std[i].Eng >= 40 && Std[i].Mat >= 40 && Std[i].Sci >= 40 &&
Std[i].Soc >= 40)
				{
					strcpy(Std[i].Res, "PASS"); //cout << "\tPASS ";

					if ( Std[i].Avg >= 90.0)
						strcpy(Std[i].Grd, "A+"); // cout << "\tA+";
					else if ( Std[i].Avg >= 80)
						strcpy(Std[i].Grd, "A2"); // cout << "\tA2";
					else if ( Std[i].Avg >= 70)
						strcpy(Std[i].Grd, "B1"); // cout << "\tB1";
					else if ( Std[i].Avg >= 60)
						strcpy(Std[i].Grd, "B2"); // cout << "\tB2";
					else if ( Std[i].Avg >= 50)
						strcpy(Std[i].Grd, "C1"); // cout << "\tC1";
					else if ( Std[i].Avg >= 40)
						strcpy(Std[i].Grd, "C2"); // cout << "\t--";
				}
				else
				{
```

```
                strcpy(Std[i].Res, "FAIL"); //cout << "\tFAIL \n";
                strcpy(Std[i].Grd, "--"); // cout << "\t--";
            }

            // AGGREGATING CLASS LEVEL
            TamTot = TamTot+ Std[i].Tam;
            EngTot = EngTot+ Std[i].Eng;
            MatTot = MatTot+ Std[i].Mat;
            SciTot = SciTot+ Std[i].Sci;
            SocTot = SocTot+ Std[i].Soc;
            TotTot = TotTot+ Std[i].Tot;
        }

        // CALCULATING SUBJECT AVERAGE
            nStd = (float) n;
            TamAvg = TamTot / nStd;
            EngAvg = EngTot / nStd;
            MatAvg = MatTot / nStd;
            SciAvg = SciTot / nStd;
            SocAvg = SocTot / nStd;
            TotAvg = TotTot / nStd;
        // SORTING STUDENTS IN DESCENDING ORDER BASED ON TOTAL MARK

        int j, Tmp;
        float Fmp;
        char Str[15];
        STUDENT sTmp;
        for(i=0; i<(n-1); i++)
        for(j=i+1; j<n; j++)
        {
// Compare two student totals; move the higher total first
            if( Std[i].Tot < Std[j].Tot)
            {
                // Exchange Student
                sTmp = Std[i];
                Std[i] = Std[j];
                Std[j] = sTmp;

            }
        }
// GENERATE THE STUDENT MARK REPORT
        cout << "\n###########################MARK REPORT BEGIN
#########################################\n";
        cout << "\nName        \tTamil  English  Maths Science Social  Total  Average  Grade  Result\n";
        for(i=0; i<n; i++)
        {
            cout <<"\n"<< Std[i].Nam <<"\t\t"<< Std[i].Tam <<"\t"<< Std[i].Eng <<"\t"<< Std[i].Mat
<<"\t"<< Std[i].Sci <<"\t"<< Std[i].Soc <<"\t"<< Std[i].Tot <<"\t"<< Std[i].Avg <<"\t"<< Std[i].Grd <<"\t"<< Std[i].Res;
        }

        cout <<
"\n##########################################################################################";
        cout <<"\n"<< "Sub Total "<<"\t"<< TamTot <<"\t"<< EngTot <<"\t"<< MatTot <<"\t"<< SciTot
<<"\t"<< SocTot <<"\t"<< TotTot;
        cout <<"\n"<< "Sub Average "<<"\t"<< TamAvg <<"\t"<< EngAvg <<"\t"<< MatAvg <<"\t"<< SciAvg
<<"\t"<< SocAvg <<"\t"<< TotAvg;
        cout << "\n######################## MARK REPORT END
#################################################";
        cin >> i;
        return 0;
    }
```

```
int getmark(char* sub)
{
        int mark;
        do{
                cout<<"\tEnter the mark of " << sub << " : ";
                cin >> mark;
                if (mark<0 || mark>100 )
                        cout <<"\nEntered " << sub << " mark is invalid" ;
        } while (mark<0 || mark>100);

        return mark;
}
```

Harsha tested the structure-based version with three students, including students who failed one or more subjects.

```
W E L C O M E, ALL THE BEST for your Learning of C
How many students need to be processed? : 3
######################################## :
      Enter the student Name[0]:Anns
      Enter the marks of Anns:
      Enter the mark of Tamil : 90
      Enter the mark of English : 40
      Enter the mark of Maths : 90
      Enter the mark of Science : 80
      Enter the mark of Social : 70
######################################## :
      Enter the student Name[1]:Mayil
      Enter the marks of Mayil:
      Enter the mark of Tamil : 90
      Enter the mark of English : 30
      Enter the mark of Maths : 40
      Enter the mark of Science : 100
      Enter the mark of Social : 100
######################################## :
      Enter the student Name[2]:Paddu
      Enter the marks of Paddu:
      Enter the mark of Tamil : 100
      Enter the mark of English : 80
      Enter the mark of Maths : 70
      Enter the mark of Science : 10
      Enter the mark of Social : 30
################## MARK INPUTS END ########################
##############################MARK REPORT BEGIN ##################################

Name       Tamil  English  Maths Science Social   Total  Average  Grade  Result
Anns          90           40     90     80     70    370    74      B1     PASS
Mayil         90           30     40    100    100    360    72      --     FAIL
Paddu        100           80     70     10     30    290    58      --     FAIL
####################################################################################
Sub Total    280          150    200    190    200   1020
Sub Average 93.33   50.0 66.66 63 63 66.66  340
########################## MARK REPORT END ##################################
```

Harsha said, “The results look correct. Shall I proceed with the full test?”
Bubesh replied, “We still need the subject-wise pass counts from our requirement checklist.”

Indu said, “Yes. We already have the marks for each student, so we can count the subject passes while processing the class.”

```
// CProg01.cpp : Defines the entry point for the console application.
//

        #include "stdafx.h"
        #include <iostream>

        using namespace std;

        // GLOBAL VARIABLES DECLARED HERE
        struct STUDENT {
                        char Nam[10];
                        int Tam;
                        int Eng;
                        int Mat;
                        int Sci;
                        int Soc;
                        int Tot;
                        float Avg;
                        char Res[10];
                        char Grd[10];
        };

        // GLOBAL FUNCTIONS OR PROTOTYPE
        //int getmark(char*);
        int getmark(char* sub)
        {
                int mark;
                do{
                        cout<<"\tEnter the mark of " << sub << " : ";
                        cin >> mark;
                        if (mark<0 || mark>100 )
                                cout <<"\nEntered " << sub << " mark is invalid" ;
                } while (mark<0 || mark>100);

                return mark;
        }

        // MAIN PROGRAM
        int _tmain(int argc, _TCHAR* argv[])
        {
                STUDENT Std[50];
                int TamTot=0, EngTot=0, MatTot=0, SciTot=0, SocTot=0, TotTot=0;
                int TamRes=0, EngRes=0, MatRes=0, SciRes=0, SocRes=0,
TotRes=0;
                float Avg[50], TamAvg,EngAvg, MatAvg, SciAvg, SocAvg, TotAvg,
nStd;
                int i,n;

                cout<<"W E L C O M E, ALL THE BEST for your Learning of C\n";

                cout << "\nHow many students need to be processed? : ";
                cin >> n;

                for(i=0; i<n; i++)
                {

                        cout << "\n############################################ : ";
                        cout << "\n\tEnter the student Name[" << i << "]:";
                        cin >> Std[i].Nam;

                        cout << "\n\tEnter the marks of " << Std[i].Nam << ":\n";
```

```
Std[i].Tam = getmark("Tamil");
Std[i].Eng = getmark("English");
Std[i].Mat = getmark("Maths");
Std[i].Sci = getmark("Science");
Std[i].Soc = getmark("Social");
}
cout << "\n################## MARK INPUTS END #######################";

// STUDENT MARK CALCULATION PROCESS DONE HERE
for(i=0; i<n; i++)
{
	Std[i].Tot = Std[i].Tam + Std[i].Eng + Std[i].Mat + Std[i].Sci +
Std[i].Soc;

	Std[i].Avg = Std[i].Tot / 5.0;

	if( Std[i].Tam>=40 && Std[i].Eng >= 40 && Std[i].Mat >= 40 && Std[i].Sci >= 40 &&
Std[i].Soc >= 40)
	{
		TotRes++;

		strcpy(Std[i].Res, "PASS"); //cout << "\tPASS ";

		if ( Std[i].Avg >= 90.0)
			strcpy(Std[i].Grd, "A+"); // cout << "\tA+";
		else if ( Std[i].Avg >= 80)
			strcpy(Std[i].Grd, "A2"); // cout << "\tA2";
		else if ( Std[i].Avg >= 70)
			strcpy(Std[i].Grd, "B1"); // cout << "\tB1";
		else if ( Std[i].Avg >= 60)
			strcpy(Std[i].Grd, "B2"); // cout << "\tB2";
		else if ( Std[i].Avg >= 50)
			strcpy(Std[i].Grd, "C1"); // cout << "\tC1";
		else if ( Std[i].Avg >= 40)
			strcpy(Std[i].Grd, "C2"); // cout << "\t--";
	}
	else
	{
		strcpy(Std[i].Res, "FAIL"); //cout << "\tFAIL \n";
		strcpy(Std[i].Grd, "--"); // cout << "\t--";
	}

	// COUNT THE NUMBER OF STUDENT PASSED IN EACH SUBJECT
	if( Std[i].Tam>=40)
		TamRes++;
	if( Std[i].Eng >= 40)
		EngRes++;
	if( Std[i].Mat >= 40)
		MatRes++;
	if( Std[i].Sci >= 40)
		SciRes++;
	if( Std[i].Soc >= 40)
		SocRes++;

	// AGGREGATING CLASS LEVEL
	TamTot = TamTot+ Std[i].Tam;
	EngTot = EngTot+ Std[i].Eng;
	MatTot = MatTot+ Std[i].Mat;
	SciTot = SciTot+ Std[i].Sci;
	SocTot = SocTot+ Std[i].Soc;
	TotTot = TotTot+ Std[i].Tot;
}
```

```
// CALCULATING SUBJECT AVERAGE
        nStd = (float) n;
        TamAvg = TamTot / nStd;
        EngAvg = EngTot / nStd;
        MatAvg = MatTot / nStd;
        SciAvg = SciTot / nStd;
        SocAvg = SocTot / nStd;
        TotAvg = TotTot / nStd;
// SORTING STUDENTS IN DESCENDING ORDER BASED ON TOTAL MARK

int j, Tmp;
float Fmp;
char Str[15];
STUDENT sTmp;
for(i=0; i<(n-1); i++)
for(j=i+1; j<n; j++)
{
        //Compare two total marks, if small than exchange it
        if( Std[i].Tot < Std[j].Tot)
        {
                // Exchange Total Mark
                sTmp = Std[i];
                Std[i] = Std[j];
                Std[j] = sTmp;

        }
}
// GENERATE THE STUDENT MARK REPORT
cout << "\n##############################MARK REPORT BEGIN
#############################################\n";
cout << "\nName        \tTamil  English  Maths Science Social  Total  Average  Grade  Result\n";
for(i=0; i<n; i++)
{
        cout <<"\n"<< Std[i].Nam <<"\t\t"<< Std[i].Tam <<"\t"<< Std[i].Eng <<"\t"<< Std[i].Mat
<<"\t"<< Std[i].Sci <<"\t"<< Std[i].Soc <<"\t"<< Std[i].Tot <<"\t"<< Std[i].Avg <<"\t"<< Std[i].Grd <<"\t"<< Std[i].Res;
}

cout <<
"\n####################################################################";
cout <<"\n"<< "Sub Total "<<"\t"<< TamTot <<"\t"<< EngTot <<"\t"<< MatTot <<"\t"<< SciTot
<<"\t"<< SocTot <<"\t"<< TotTot;
cout <<"\n"<< "Sub Average "<<"\t"<< TamAvg <<"\t"<< EngAvg <<"\t"<< MatAvg <<"\t"<< SciAvg
<<"\t"<< SocAvg <<"\t"<< TotAvg;
cout <<"\n"<< "Sub Result "<<"\t"<< TamRes <<"\t"<< EngRes <<"\t"<< MatRes <<"\t"<< SciRes
<<"\t"<< SocRes <<"\t"<< TotRes;
cout << "\n########################### MARK REPORT END
##############################################";
cin >> i;
return 0;
    }
```

Harsha tested the updated version.

```
W E L C O M E, ALL THE BEST for your Learning of C
How many students need to be processed? : 3
######################################## :
     Enter the student Name[0]:Anns
     Enter the marks of Anns:
     Enter the mark of Tamil : 90
     Enter the mark of English : 40
     Enter the mark of Maths : 90
     Enter the mark of Science : 80
```

```
    Enter the mark of Social : 70
######################################## :
    Enter the student Name[1]:Mayil
    Enter the marks of Mayil:
    Enter the mark of Tamil : 90
    Enter the mark of English : 30
    Enter the mark of Maths : 40
    Enter the mark of Science : 100
    Enter the mark of Social : 100
######################################## :
    Enter the student Name[2]:Paddu
    Enter the marks of Paddu:
    Enter the mark of Tamil : 100
    Enter the mark of English : 80
    Enter the mark of Maths : 70
    Enter the mark of Science : 10
    Enter the mark of Social : 30
################## MARK INPUTS END ########################
############################MARK REPORT BEGIN ##################################
Name      Tamil English   Maths Science   Social  Total Average Grade  Result
Anns        90    40     90      80               70   370   74                 B1    PASS
Mayil       90    30     40     100              100   360   72     --    FAIL
Paddu      100    80     70      10               30   290   58               --     FAIL
##################################################################################
Sub Total     280    150    200    190    200    1020
Sub Average 93.33  33.50 66.66 67.63 66.66  340
Sub Result    3            2      3      2     2            1
########################### MARK REPORT END ###################################
```

Thea reviewed the changes and the test results. "Good work. Notice what happened after you introduced the structure. Earlier, exchanging two students required you to swap every related field separately. Now the same operation can be expressed by exchanging two complete STUDENT records. The code is shorter, clearer and easier to maintain."

Earlier approach — exchanging each field separately:

```
for(i=0; i<(n-1); i++)
for(j=i+1; j<n; j++)
{
        //Compare two total marks, if small than exchange it
        if( Tot[i] < Tot[j])
        {
                // Exchange Total Mark
                Tmp = Tot[i];
                Tot[i] = Tot[j];
                Tot[j] = Tmp;

                // Exchange Tamil Mark
                Tmp = Tam[i];
                Tam[i] = Tam[j];
                Tam[j] = Tmp;

                // Exchange English Mark
                Tmp = Eng[i];
                Eng[i] = Eng[j];
                Eng[j] = Tmp;

                // Exchange Maths Mark
                Tmp = Mat[i];
                Mat[i] = Mat[j];
                Mat[j] = Tmp;
```

```
                                        // Exchange Science Mark
                                        Tmp = Sci[i];
                                        Sci[i] = Sci[j];
                                        Sci[j] = Tmp;

                                        // Exchange Total Mark
                                        Tmp = Soc[i];
                                        Soc[i] = Soc[j];
                                        Soc[j] = Tmp;

                                        // Exchange Average Mark
                                        Fmp = Avg[i];
                                        Avg[i] = Avg[j];
                                        Avg[j] = Fmp;

                                        // Exchange the Name
                                        strcpy(Str, Nam[i]);
                                        strcpy(Nam[i], Nam[j]);
                                        strcpy(Nam[j], Str);
                                        // Exchange the Res
                                        strcpy(Str, Res[i]);
                                        strcpy(Res[i], Res[j]);
                                        strcpy(Res[j], Str);

                                        // Exchange the Grade
                                        strcpy(Str, Grd[i]);
                                        strcpy(Grd[i], Grd[j]);
                                        strcpy(Grd[j], Str);
                                }
                        }
```

Improved approach — exchanging the complete STUDENT record:

```
                        for(i=0; i<(n-1); i++)
                        for(j=i+1; j<n; j++)
                        {
// Compare two student totals; move the higher total first
                                if( Std[i].Tot < Std[j].Tot)
                                {
// Exchange the complete student record
                                        sTmp = Std[i];
                                        Std[i] = Std[j];
                                        Std[j] = sTmp;
                                }
                        }
```

Thea continued, “We could also group some of the class-level totals and statistics into another structure. But do not introduce a new concept merely to reduce a few lines. The present design is clear enough for this stage. The results look satisfactory, so the next important step is user testing with CK Sir.”

All three thanked Thea for the review.

Testing the Improved Design

Harsha wanted stronger evidence before the demonstration, so he expanded the test data to fifteen students. He deliberately included passes, failures, boundary values and an invalid mark to verify the input validation.

```
W E L C O M E, ALL THE BEST for your Learning of C
How many students need to be processed? : 15
#################################### :
```

```
        Enter the student Name[0]:Anns
        Enter the marks of Anns:
        Enter the mark of Tamil : 90
        Enter the mark of English : 60
        Enter the mark of Maths : 100
        Enter the mark of Science : 70
        Enter the mark of Social : 50
######################################## :
        Enter the student Name[1]:Mayil
        Enter the marks of Mayil:
        Enter the mark of Tamil : 90
        Enter the mark of English : 50
        Enter the mark of Maths : 100
        Enter the mark of Science : 20
        Enter the mark of Social : 100
######################################## :
        Enter the student Name[2]:Paddu
        Enter the marks of Paddu:
        Enter the mark of Tamil : 99
        Enter the mark of English : 100
        Enter the mark of Maths : 100
        Enter the mark of Science : 33
        Enter the mark of Social : 40
######################################## :
        Enter the student Name[3]:Senthil
        Enter the marks of Senthil:
        Enter the mark of Tamil : 80
        Enter the mark of English : 10
        Enter the mark of Maths : 100
        Enter the mark of Science : 100
        Enter the mark of Social : 10
######################################## :
        Enter the student Name[4]:Suku
        Enter the marks of Suku:
        Enter the mark of Tamil : 10
        Enter the mark of English : 99
        Enter the mark of Maths : 100
        Enter the mark of Science : 80
        Enter the mark of Social : 10
######################################## :
        Enter the student Name[5]:Thea
        Enter the marks of Thea:
        Enter the mark of Tamil : 90
        Enter the mark of English : 70
        Enter the mark of Maths : 100
        Enter the mark of Science : 44
        Enter the mark of Social : 55
######################################## :
        Enter the student Name[6]:Deerdya
        Enter the marks of Deerdya:
        Enter the mark of Tamil : 90
        Enter the mark of English : 40
        Enter the mark of Maths : 100
        Enter the mark of Science : 100
        Enter the mark of Social : 88
######################################## :
        Enter the student Name[7]:Sruthi
        Enter the marks of Sruthi:
        Enter the mark of Tamil : 90
        Enter the mark of English : 50
        Enter the mark of Maths : 100
        Enter the mark of Science : 60
```

```
      Enter the mark of Social : 100
######################################## :
      Enter the student Name[8]:Magadhi
      Enter the marks of Magadhi:
      Enter the mark of Tamil : 100
      Enter the mark of English : 30
      Enter the mark of Maths : 100
      Enter the mark of Science : 100
      Enter the mark of Social : 100
######################################## :
      Enter the student Name[9]:Kousal
      Enter the marks of Kousal:
      Enter the mark of Tamil : 40
      Enter the mark of English : 90
      Enter the mark of Maths : 100
      Enter the mark of Science : 100
      Enter the mark of Social : 40
######################################## :
      Enter the student Name[10]:Akil
      Enter the marks of Akil:
      Enter the mark of Tamil : 90
      Enter the mark of English : 99
      Enter the mark of Maths : 100
      Enter the mark of Science : 87
      Enter the mark of Social : 05
######################################## :
      Enter the student Name[11]:Ramulu
      Enter the marks of Ramulu:
      Enter the mark of Tamil : 99
      Enter the mark of English : 77
      Enter the mark of Maths : 100
      Enter the mark of Science : 100
      Enter the mark of Social : 70
######################################## :
      Enter the student Name[12]:Krish
      Enter the marks of Krish:
      Enter the mark of Tamil : 90
      Enter the mark of English : 60
      Enter the mark of Maths : 50
      Enter the mark of Science : 100
      Enter the mark of Social : 87
######################################## :
      Enter the student Name[13]:Sindu
      Enter the marks of Sindu:
      Enter the mark of Tamil : 100
      Enter the mark of English : 90
      Enter the mark of Maths : 100
      Enter the mark of Science : 100
      Enter the mark of Social : 60
######################################## :
      Enter the student Name[14]:Harsha
      Enter the marks of Harsha:
      Enter the mark of Tamil : 988
Entered Tamil mark is invalid   Enter the mark of Tamil : 98
      Enter the mark of English : 100
      Enter the mark of Maths : 100
      Enter the mark of Science : 100
      Enter the mark of Social : 56
################## MARK INPUTS END ########################
###########################MARK REPORT BEGIN ##############################################
Name      Tamil     English    Maths      Science    Social    Total     Average   Grade     Result
###########################################################################################
Harsha        98    100                   100        100       56        454       90.8      A+        PASS
```

```
Sindu        100          90   100   100    60   450   90     A+    PASS
Ramulu        99          77   100   100    70   446   89.2   A2    PASS
Magadhi      100          30   100   100   100   430   86     --    FAIL
Deerdya       90          40   100   100    88   418   83.6   A2    PASS
Sruthi        90          50   100    60   100   400   80     A2    PASS
Krish         90          60    50   100    87   387   77.4   B1    PASS
Akil          90          99   100    87     5   381   76.2   --    FAIL
Paddu         99    100  100    33    40   372   74.4    --   FAIL
Kousal        40          90   100   100    40   370   74     B1    PASS
Anns          90          60   100    70    50   370   74     B1    PASS
Mayil         90          50   100    20   100   360   72     --    FAIL
Thea          90          70   100    44    55   359   71.8   B1    PASS
Senthil       80          10   100   100    10   300   60     --    FAIL
Suku          10          99   100    80    10   299   59.8   --    FAIL
##########################################################################################
Sub Total    1256        1025   1450   1194   871   5796
Sub Average 83.73        68.33  96.66  67 79  58.06  386.4
Sub Result    14          13     15     13     12     9
############################ MARK REPORT END ##############################################
```

The larger test produced the expected ordering, pass/fail decisions, subject totals, averages and pass counts. Harsha still wanted to keep testing, but the team now had enough confidence to demonstrate the program to CK Sir and RC Sir the next morning.

They ended the evening satisfied with their progress, though naturally a little nervous about demonstrating their work in front of their teachers.

PART VII — FROM PROJECT TO PRODUCT

Demonstrate → Pilot → Verify → Improve

Demonstrating the Solution

The next morning, after tea, all three assembled in the staff room with the laptop. CK Sir, RC Sir and several other class teachers had gathered for the demonstration.

Seeing so many teachers increased the students' nervousness. CK Sir and RC Sir encouraged them and reminded them that the program had already passed many of their tests.

Bubesh began the demonstration by explaining the problem they had observed, the requirements they had collected and the solution they had built. Indu demonstrated the program, while Harsha explained the testing and stepped in whenever questions arose. At the end, the teachers applauded their work. Hearing the applause, Headmaster Sriramulu Sir entered the staff room and asked about the project.

The Headmaster (HM) asked, "What benefits does this program provide?"

CK Sir explained, "Preparing progress reports manually takes several hours each month. This program can reduce much of that repeated calculation and reporting effort. It can also improve consistency by automating calculations, although the results still need to be verified carefully during the initial use."

The HM asked, "Very good. Can other classes use it too?"

CK Sir replied, "The design is reusable for classes that follow the same five-subject pattern. RC Sir can explain the present limitation."

RC Sir said, "At this stage the program assumes exactly five subjects. That works for the classes following this pattern, but classes with a different number of subjects would require a modification. A better next step would be to make the number and names of subjects configurable."

HM Sriramulu Sir said, "If several class teachers can each save a few hours of repetitive work every month, the combined time benefit to the school could be substantial. That time can be used for teaching, student support and other valuable work."

CK Sir replied, "Yes, sir. The students identified that benefit when they first observed the problem. More importantly, they have learned how to turn a real need into a working solution."

The HM said, "Wonderful. Once the program is sufficiently verified, I would like the school to begin using it."

Pilot, Parallel Verification and Feedback

Here is the corrected and polished version of your text:
RC Sir added, "I recommend a parallel run first. For one or two reporting cycles, teachers should prepare the existing manual results while also running the program. We can then compare both outputs. If we find any defects or missing requirements, we can correct them before relying on the software."

HM Sriramulu Sir agreed. “That is a sensible approach. We will ask a small number of class teachers to pilot it first.”

He then asked, “How long would it take to make the program work for classes with a different number of subjects?”

The project team discussed it briefly with RC Sir. Indu replied, “We understand the direction, but we should first redesign it carefully and test it, rather than promise a fixed deadline before studying the required changes.”

The Headmaster smiled. “Good answer. I appreciate both your enthusiasm and your caution.” CK Sir said, “These students deserve appreciation for identifying a real problem and developing a useful solution.”

Headmaster Sriramulu Sir replied, “Certainly. I will mention the project during tomorrow’s school assembly. I also want the students to explain not only the program but what they learned from observing the problem, working as a team, testing for mistakes, and improving the solution.”

Bubesh said, “Sir, Thea was instrumental in helping us choose the direction of the project. CK Sir and RC Sir guided us throughout the development. Please include them when you speak about the project.”

The Headmaster replied, “I appreciate that you remembered everyone who contributed. We will acknowledge their guidance.”

RC Sir added, “Meanwhile, CK Sir can select a couple of class teachers for the pilot. We will collect their feedback and review any improvements with the project team.” The teachers applauded again, and a few students who had gathered near the staff room joined in.

The three friends walked out of the staff room proud of what they had achieved—but they also understood that a successful demonstration was not the end of software development.

LEARNING POINT — A successful demo proves that a solution is promising; it does not prove that it is defect-free. Real users, parallel verification and feedback are part of turning a project into dependable software.

They shared the news with Thea. She congratulated them warmly.

Thea asked, "Did the teachers suggest any improvements?"

Removing Fixed Assumptions

Harsha replied, "Yes. The present program assumes five subjects, so it cannot directly handle every class. Should we write a separate program for classes with a different number of subjects?"

Thea replied, "You could, but that would create another fixed program. If the school changes the subjects again later, you would have to modify or create yet another version for each class. That would increase code maintenance difficulties and make it hard to keep them in sync. A better design is to make a generic program that accepts the number of subjects and their names as input data."

Bubesh asked, "How can we do that?"

Thea explained, "You already ask for the number of students. In the same way, the program can ask for the number of subjects. Instead of keeping separate variables named Tamil, English, Maths, and so on, you can store the subject names and marks in arrays. Then, the same logic can process different subject combinations without changing the source code each time."

Indu said, "That makes sense. The requirement has changed, so our data design must become more general. I will study the available options, and we can redesign it together."

Thea replied, "Excellent. This is how useful software grows. You solve one problem, people use the solution, feedback reveals new needs, and the next improvement begins. Congratulations—and keep learning."

Indu, Bubesh, and Harsha replied together, "Thank you so much, Thea."

```
W E L C O M E, ALL THE BEST for your Learning of C
How many students need to be processed? : 5
############################################ :
    Enter the student Name[0]:Jenifer
    Enter the mark of Tamil : 90
    Enter the mark of English : 23
    Enter the mark of Maths : 55
    Enter the mark of Science : 66
    Enter the mark of Social : 77
############################################ :
    Enter the student Name[1]:Raghu
    Enter the mark of Tamil : 90
    Enter the mark of English : 67
    Enter the mark of Maths : 99
    Enter the mark of Science : 56
```

```
    Enter the mark of Social : 87
############################################ :
    Enter the student Name[2]:Sen
    Enter the mark of Tamil : 99
    Enter the mark of English : 55
    Enter the mark of Maths : 66
    Enter the mark of Science : 55
    Enter the mark of Social : 66
############################################ :
    Enter the student Name[3]:Suku
    Enter the mark of Tamil : 86
    Enter the mark of English : 45
    Enter the mark of Maths : 65
    Enter the mark of Science : 77
    Enter the mark of Social : 55
############################################ :
    Enter the student Name[4]:Muru
    Enter the mark of Tamil : 45
    Enter the mark of English : 30
    Enter the mark of Maths : 40
    Enter the mark of Science : 230
Entered Science mark is invalid Enter the mark of Science : 23
    Enter the mark of Social : 28
################## MARK INPUTS END ########################
###############################MARK REPORT BEGIN ##############################################
Name      Tamil  English  Maths        Science   Social      Total      Average    Grade      Result
##############################################################################################################
Raghu        90       67      99      56          87          399        79             B1    PASS
Sen           99       55      66      55          66          341        68             B2    PASS
Suku         86       45      65      77          55          328        65             B2    PASS
Jenifer      90       23      55      66          77          311        62             --               FAIL
Muru         45       30      40      23          28          166        33             --               FAIL
##############################################################################################################
Sub Total      401   220   325         277         313          1545
Sub Average : 82.2  44.0  65.0         55.4        62.6         309.0
Sub Result :     5     3     5          4           4               3
############################ MARK REPORT END ############################################
```

The Journey Continues

When there is a change, we need to ensure that the new system works and meets its purpose by running both systems simultaneously. Once confirmed, the school will drop the old system and fully transition to the new one, a process known as "**cutover**."

Therefore, the HM decided to complete the agreed two-months parallel run, which could even be tested using historical data from completed months. For those two reporting cycles, the selected class teachers prepared their reports in the usual manual way and also processed the same marks using the students' program.

Two Months Later — Feedback from Real Use

At the end of the second month, CK Sir and the other teachers met with the project team again.

They had compared the computer-generated results with the manually prepared reports. The totals, averages, pass/fail decisions, grades, and rankings matched their verified records.

Most importantly, the teachers reported that the repetitive calculation and report-preparation work had been reduced substantially.

CK Sir said, "The program has now been used with real class data for two reporting cycles. It has saved us a considerable amount of time, and the parallel verification has given us confidence in the calculations. The time we save can be used for teaching and supporting students."

Harsha asked, "Then is our project complete, Sir?"

CK Sir smiled. "This stage is complete. But while using it, we noticed the next improvement. Every reporting cycle, we still have to enter the students' names and related details again. Those details do not change every month. Why should we repeatedly type the same information?"

Bubesh replied, "Then we should enter each student's details once and reuse them whenever marks are processed."

RC Sir said, "Exactly. Until now, most of the information in your program lives only while the program is running. To reuse student information next month—or even after the computer is restarted—you need to store it permanently. That takes us into a new area: files and persistent data."

A New Door Opens — Files and Persistent Data

Thea explained, “This is an important boundary for this project. You began with arithmetic, conditions, and loops; then, you used functions, arrays, and structures to build a useful application. File handling adds another dimension: the program can remember information beyond a single execution.”

She continued, “A future version could maintain a Student Master containing information such as admission number, roll number, name, class, and other student details. Monthly marks could then be recorded against those existing students, instead of entering the same details repeatedly. From there, the system could grow further into searching records, updating student information, promotion to the next class, and historical reports.”

Indu said, “So, our first project has finished on a positive note. When a piece of work is utilized well, it naturally brings more requests and further enhancements. This means it has succeeded enough for the users to ask for the next improvement.”

RC Sir replied, “Exactly. That is one of the best signs of useful software. Real use creates real feedback, and real feedback shows what should be built next.”

LEARNING POINT — Observe → Build → Test → Use → Get Feedback → Improve

The project that began with a teacher, a calculator, and a pile of report cards had now become a working learning journey. The students had not merely learned C statements; they had learned how to observe a problem, convert it into requirements, build a solution step by step, make mistakes, debug them, test with real data, listen to users, and improve the design.

For now, this is where our story pauses. File handling and persistent student records are deliberately left as the next major learning journey. After this book is used by learners and teachers, their feedback will help decide how that next journey should be shaped.

A working program is not the end of learning. It is evidence that we are ready for the next problem...

Made in the USA
Coppell, TX
04 November 2026

11287993R00050